DISCERNMENT
THROUGH PARABLES AND STORIES

Deacon Ray Biersbach, PhD

ISBN 978-1-66783-586-0 eBook 978-1-66783-587-7

THE CATHOLIC PSYCHOTHERAPY ASSOCIATION (CPA)

Its mission is to support mental health practitioners by promoting the development of psychological theory and mental health practice which encompasses a full understanding of the human person, family, and society in fidelity to the Magisterium of the Catholic Church.

Thanks, and acknowledgments to:

James Jasper, Illustrator

Readers:

My thanks to the readers who made this a better book.

The readers include
Geri Biersbach, my wife
Ray Biersbach, M.D., my son
Tom Biersbach, my brother
Deacon Gene Vanderzanden, my fellow deacon
Arthur Sullivan, Ph.D., my longtime friend.

CONTENTS

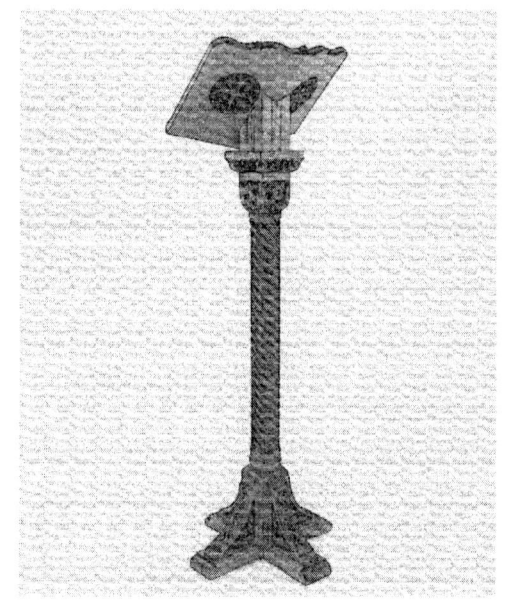

Figure 1

As we begin.

James Joyce

PSYCHOLOGICAL AND SPIRITUAL DISCERNMENT

Discernment is the ability to obtain sharp perceptions or judge well. People prize it in psychological, moral, aesthetic, or spiritual domains. Discernment is essential in defining scientific, normative, or conventional terms.

Two paths will lead us into and through discernment. ACT (Acceptance and Commitment Therapy) will give the psychological perspective, and Jesus' parables will provide the theological material for reflection.

ACT is a current approach that has emerged out of the CBT (cognitive-behavior therapy) tradition. ACT encourages flexibility in responding to life stressors and approaching problems rather than avoiding them. Worksheet #1, ACT's six therapeutic processes, offers a brief outline of the core ACT processes. It is an approach that will help link some of the psychological elements in psychotherapy with faith elements.

As for the theological and faith elements, I propose turning to Jesus' parables. His parables are stories. The Bible is full of an intriguing variety of stories. The Old Testament, for example, is awash in similes, comparisons, and parables (Snodgrass, 2018, pp. 38-42, 168), for example, 2 Kings (19:30), Isaiah (27:6, 37:31, 43:5, 60:21), Jeremiah (24:5-7, 31:27-28), Ezekiel 36:9, Hosea 14:5, and Ezra 8:41-44.

Jesus is a masterful storyteller who moved effortlessly from simile to comparisons to parables, analogies, metaphors, and what Jeremias (1963, pp. 227-229) calls parabolic actions. His parables are about a third of his recorded teaching.

His parables, I assert, are a most helpful approach to learning about the elements of discernment. Jesus' strategy was to use figures of speech and tales with seamless relevance to questions asked. Similarly, psychotherapists begin with clients by first listening to their clients' stories and then reflecting on and making sense of those stories with clinical supervisors.

For example, in the parable of **Matthew's five wise and five foolish young women** (25:1-13), the girls' task was simple. According to Jewish custom, their job was to provide light at the nighttime wedding celebration (Wenham, 1989, pp. 80-82). They each had the required lamp to do their job, but only half had foresight enough to bring oil for their light (Snodgrass, 2018, pp. 517-518). Those who brought oil showed good judgment and preparedness. Similarly, discernment and preparation are positive traits for anyone. However, there is a particular need for discernment and preparation for psychotherapists working with clients. That's what being a competent CPA therapist implies.

The discerning individual does not tolerate any attempt to mooch off others as the five foolish young women did, rather than embracing personal responsibility. Psychotherapists share a similar personal responsibility to develop our ability to discern and prepare for work with clients (Blomberg, 2012, p. 244).

Hopefully, this book will act as a conversation starter for those reflecting on psychological and spiritual discernment.

For the professional psychotherapist and Catholic Christian, the question is what evidence is there that linking research-based psychotherapy and lived Catholic values is a worthwhile undertaking?

ACT is a preeminent research-based approach to psychotherapy. Though ACT is only about 35 years old, it is a robust updating of the CBT (cognitive-behavior therapy) tradition. In empirical research, it has the advantage of working at ALL educational levels. Wide-ranging research indicates that it works well trans-nationally (Hayes S. , Common Misunderstandings About ACT/ RFT).

However, what about a manageable approach to the vast field of lived Catholic values?

Hankle's (2013) article described many obstacles to the operational definition of "lived Catholic values" when thinking about training psychotherapists to assist clients in discerning God's intentions for their lives.

First, the understanding of Christian anthropology is shared to varying degrees by many Christian traditions. However, the Catholic sense of Christian personhood has taken on a distinct character over time, especially in virtue philosophy, which will be one of this book's themes.

Second, Hankle noted that dealing with spiritual issues is too often confined to spiritual direction, which has become a distinct discipline. The similarities and differences in approach between spiritual direction and psychotherapy have been explored in my book on religious experience (Biersbach, 2021). Psychotherapists have different training needs than those trained in the traditional understanding of spiritual direction and discernment.

Hankle identified a further difficulty, namely, "clinical programs are burdened with professional requirements and often lack the time to educate students in spiritual aspects of clinical work." Training in religious/spiritual issues and discernment done for clergy over many years of philosophy and theology is impossible for clinicians due to time constraints. Nor is a long period of living in a vowed community possible for psychotherapists, primarily lay men and women.

Discernment and the biblical stories offer psychotherapists formation opportunities in spiritual and religious discernment. Understanding how that can be effective depends on stepping back a bit and putting the role of the laity into a biblical perspective.

To illustrate that, please try a thought experiment with me. Pretend that you know absolutely nothing about the long and messy history of inspired canonicity, that is, how over four millennia the faithful discerned what books to put in the Bible and how best to organize them.

It takes only a glance at the table of contents of any bible to see that both the Old Testament (OT) and New Testament (NT) can be looked at as made up of three traditions: the historical/priestly, the prophetic, and the wisdom/lay tradition.

The priestly tradition emerged in the historical books in the OT. In the NT the priestly tradition emerged in the Gospels plus Acts.

The prophetic tradition is recorded, except for Elijah and Eisha, in the OT prophetic books. In the NT the letters of St. Paul and his disciples are the preeminent prophets of the new age.

We may not think of St. Paul as a prophet. However, Redditt (2012, pp. 588-590) wrote that the OT refers to prophets as "nabi" or those who deliver a message. Paul certainly delivered an abundance of messages!

The OT also called prophets men of God with a distinct call from God, and both descriptors also apply to St. Paul.

Further, like the OT prophets, Paul was clear that his sources were not his reflection on the life and teaching of Jesus. As scholars point out, he barely mentioned the life or sayings of the historical Jesus. Instead, Paul spoke of the resurrected Christ who appeared to him at least three times: on the road to Damascus (Acts 9:4-5), in ecstasy in the temple (Acts 22:17-21), and a vision in prison (Acts 23:11). Perhaps even more startling, he asserted that his understanding of the mysteries of the Christian life was from personal revelation by the Holy Spirit (Ephesians 3:2-3a, 5-6) rather than because of his Talmudic training or brilliant insight of the kinds the wisdom authors presume.

The OT wisdom or lay tradition consists of the five novella—Tobit, Judith, Esther, and 1st and 2nd Maccabees—plus the other wisdom books.

In the NT, Jesus does it all. As Hebrews wrote, Jesus is priest, prophet, and king. The priestly tradition is, of course, continued in the Gospels, and the prophetic in St. Paul. The wisdom tradition in the NT is the Catholic letters, saints Peter, Jude, James, and John. Even Revelation is a long letter from St. John in exile on Patmos to the seven cities in his diocese.

Over the last two millennia, those three traditions each have had their history within the life of the Church. However, focusing on the wisdom of the parables and the wisdom tradition generally, this reflection has a "feel" from many apostolic/priestly works that tend to focus more clearly on doctrinal truth or Church unity and good order. It also reads quite markedly different from the prophetic tradition, historically linked to the life of vowed religious communities, with their praiseworthy emphasis on their mission, prompted by God, to meet the needs of some neglected group.

Throughout, our focus will be to attend to three kinds of narrative: 1) the Biblical stories, especially Jesus' parables, 2) client stories and 3) our own stories. The parables of Jesus and other tales in the Bible will guide us spiritually. Current psychotherapy research, especially ACT, with its insight into the human psyche will guide us psychologically.

Our stories remain crucial and point us toward reflecting on our stories.

Therefore, please indulge me by doing a thought experiment. Open a bible and pretend that you know nothing about it. Go to the table of contents and see how believers divided the OT and NT into the historical, prophetic, and wisdom books. All are essential, and I propose, equally important but in uniquely different ways.

For example, prophetic books engage a unique pattern of disorientation, amazement, and reorientation (Brueggemann, 1985). By comparison, the priestly tradition might be condensed into a lead, teach, celebrate pattern.

However, the wisdom narratives follow a pattern of music, drama, wise sayings, stories of fearless women, romances, witnessing in suffering, plus the love of art, beauty, and passion to order, disorder, and reorder (Rohr, 2001, 2020).

To undo spiritual boredom, begin looking for one verse or a story from the prophetic or wisdom books and hear how the Spirit spoke then and speaks to us now.

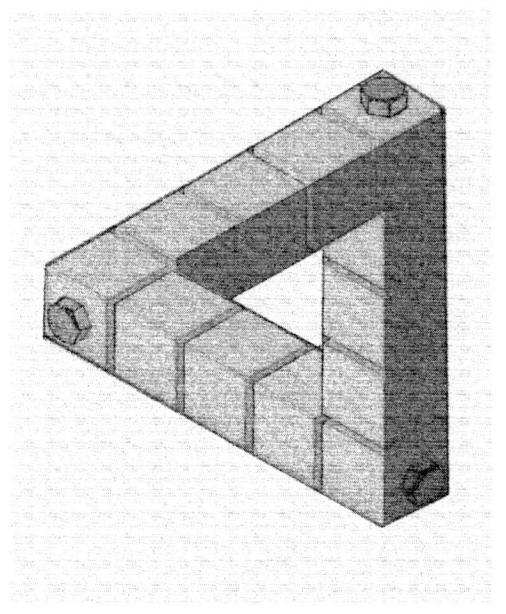

Figure 2

Parables as paradox.

James Jasper

2

TOWARD COMPETENT DISCERNMENT FOR PSYCHOTHERAPISTS

The Catholic understanding of discernment is the quality of grasping and comprehending the complexities of religious experiences. But for the psychotherapist, discernment is also the ability to make an informed assessment and diagnosis of client behavior.

Further, in both the spiritual and psychological fields, the discernment task is to separate what is essential and genuine and what is not. While the criteria for clinicians are references such as the DSM-5, the standard for Christians is an authentic search for God's will. Both psychological and spiritual perspectives presume that discernment applies to social, moral, vocational, and personality issues.

I presume that Catholic psychotherapists are interested in both spiritual and psychological discernment. The question then is how CPA (Catholic Psychotherapy Association) might foster the growth of discernment skills.

CPA members are typically well-formed academically through multiple years of graduate school academic training and through additional years of clinical supervision. This book holds up the use of stories and parables as a way to develop discernment skills through linking the best of psychotherapy and the best of spirituality.

The priestly and vowed religious traditions have worked out distinct pathways in forming their membership. Those in the priestly tradition typically include two years of college-level philosophy and four years of graduate-level theology. By comparison, supervision, and formation for vowed religious typically occur both academically and within a community setting over many years.

Neither six years of academic philosophy and theology nor a years-long commitment to a community of vowed religious is within reach for most practicing psychotherapists.

Hegy (2017, p. 163) proposed membership in a charismatic group as a means of lay formation. However, the prophetic is a three-step process: disorientation, amazement, and reorientation (Brueggemann, 2018). The prophetic voice presumes a skill set no charismatic prayer group I have been in can impart. Instead, the prophetic stance is an anointing of the Spirit. True prophecy can "nurture, nourish, and evoke a consciousness and perception alternative to the consciousness and perception of the dominant culture around us" (Brueggemann, 2018, p. 3).

Both academic graduate degrees in philosophy or theology or participation in a charismatic prayer group can be helpful and valuable. However, both are echoes of the clerical and vowed religious traditions, and as mentioned, the time demands of psychotherapy training preclude the possibility for most. Accordingly, I hypothesize that CPA psychotherapists will do well to look to the more distinctly wisdom strains in the Bible.

Jesus is normative for Christians, and thus he is our model in discerning (Catechism #520). More specifically, his use of parables offers a good standard for psychotherapists. To access the riches of the parables, let us reflect on the narrative or storytelling tradition in the Bible.

Sternberg (1985) wrote that biblical narrative speaks directly to listeners like all social conversations. For example, people asked Jesus about 150 questions in the Gospels, and he gave about 300 answers. The question-and-answer format still grabs us, and we remain in suspense until we hear and evaluate the response. As an art form, that power to grab our attention tends to be timeless. When we read or hear the question, we enter the time and age of the narrator.

That grasp of our attention is very like a client's recounting of their tale that also leads the client and the psychotherapist to re-enter that period in the client's life.

Sternberg (p. 1-2) continued that in narrative biblical accounts, the emphasis is on the text and the power of the story to grip us and less on the historical reality. The standard for narrative is the standard of fiction. Namely, does it ring accurate, not in the observable world, but is it authentic in the fictional realm that the story has created? Effective psychotherapists listen to clients throughout therapy with an openness that facilitates sharing (p. 6). In similar fashion, stories open our inner selves to reflecting on the dynamics of our personal journeys through life.

Narrative storytelling is a discourse-oriented approach, as is psychotherapy (p. 23). Art and insight regulate storytelling (p. 41) rather than orderly logic and slavishly recounting every detail. Values dictate what to include or exclude.

The styles of each biblical tradition vary based on their focus, range of concern, and values. For example, the apostolic/priestly tradition might connect and present the past revelation and focus attention on the credal language. The prophetic focus leans toward face-to-face pronouncements and explicitly denies ever being part of the company of wisdom sages or speaking based on reflection or speculation (Shields, 2008, p. 880). By comparison, the wisdom narrative communicates through written storytelling without explicitly identifying the author or the audience (Sternberg, 1985, p. 58). Wisdom aims for skills in living well, whereas prophecy gives direct and specific information from God addressing a particular situation (Shields, 2008, p. 877).

An advantage of storytelling is that the biblical narrator seamlessly has access to God's intentions, infinite knowledge, and human subjects' hearts and minds. In storytelling, God's firm hold on the truth stands out in direct proportion to the narrator's blindness, wonder, stumbling, and mystification. Ideally, the narrator's exterior and interior rhetoric are balanced, neither over nor under dramatizing (Sternberg, 1985, pp. 85-87).

Sternberg added that God's role in biblical storytelling is as an inspiring originator, guiding through the individual perspective of some human subject (p. 153). In content, the biblical narrative repeatedly traces the movement from unhappiness to happiness, from ignorance to knowledge and insight, and universally creates a tension between limited human understanding and the unrestricted understanding of God (p. 172-173). The biblical narratives illustrate the partial knowledge of humans versus the infinite knowledge of God (p. 235). In biblical storytelling, the message is always divine, and the messenger is always human.

As in forensic psychological assessment, where it is often helpful to ask, "And then what?" the biblical narratives leave us guessing at each step, "What will happen next? and "How will it relate to what has already happened?" That dynamic is omnipresent in Jesus' responses to the questions put to him (Sternberg, 1985, p. 186).

Remarkably, the delicate telling, and sophistication of the biblical narratives feature approaches undreamt of before modernism (p. 230). In art, as in life, suspense derives from incomplete knowledge. Further, the biblical narratives use expectant restlessness, awareness of gaps, gap-filling descriptions that often conflict, and the movement toward some point of resolution while never overdoing or underdoing the level of suspense (p. 264-265).

As Henry James put it, "the whole of anything is never told, but the whole of anything is never suppressed." Biblical narratives use gaps and omissions most masterfully, and the reader must piece the story together from dramatic givens in a process like the Rorschach projective test (p. 321-322). Additionally, for example, Jesus used repetition in the three parables about fig-trees but led to a distinct point in each one (p. 365).

Finally, the literary court takes place in the court of conscience rather than in rigid legal or social settings.

What is new in all this for our day and time? One answer is that Jesus' parables illustrate concerns parallel to the current ACT

(Acceptance and Commitment Therapy) approaches (Hayes S. , The Six Core Processes of ACT), namely,

1. ACT teaches acceptance of inner and outer experience rather than avoidance, escape, or responding only to events that a client can control. Such is the case in the behavior of the priest and the Levite in the **Good Samaritan** (Luke 10:25-37) story.

2. ACT teaches observation of our thoughts, feelings, and actions rather than impulsively acting. Jesus repeatedly urged observation over impulsive judgment in his parables.

3. ACT affirms the present moment rather than focusing on memories of the past or fears about the future. Jesus also called his hearers to consider their status before God in the present moment.

4. ACT fosters a sense of self that says that being a person is more than one's thoughts, feelings, and actions. Jesus called us to respond to his kingdom beyond momentary changes in our feelings and thoughts.

5. ACT urges clarification of values and attention to what results from values or the lack of values. Jesus also supported values clarification in the service of producing fruit for his kingdom.

6. ACT facilitates clients putting professed values into practice both for the present and the future. Jesus' story of the Good Samaritan's action toward the robbery victim has a similar point. The other two who passed by may have professed care for others, but the Samaritan acted on those values.

7. ACT's overriding principle is flexibility in applying values rather than acting on social expectations or fixed roles. Jesus' responses to questions were likewise flexible in pointing to the need to exceed

social expectations if his hearers were to become his followers.

The biblical parable of **the Good Samaritan** (Luke 10:25-37) has three lessons (Blomberg, 2012, pp. 301-302), namely, that 1) from the example of the priest and Levite comes the principle that religious status or legalistic casuistry does not excuse love-lessness. 2) From the Samaritan one learns that one must show compassion to those in dire need regardless of the religious or ethnic barriers that divide people. 3) From the man in the ditch emerges the lesson that even one's enemy is one's neighbor.

Snodgrass (2018, pp. 344-345) added, "Jews believed Samaritans to be people of doubtful descent and inadequate theology," a condescending judgment still too often pinned on groups and individuals.

In this parable, Jesus praised the questioner, an attorney, for his correct answer. However, as the biblical author noted, the attorney, to prove how very right he was, asked who he was legally obligated to consider his neighbor. Jesus' approach in the story was to indicate the limits of the vision of the priest and the Levite.

Q1: Lawyer: What must I do to inherit eternal life?

A1: Jesus: do as the Samaritan did.

Q2: Lawyer: how do you read what is written in the law?

A2: Jesus: Love God and neighbor.

Q3: Lawyer: who is my neighbor?

A3: Jesus: define neighbor as the Samaritan did.

Q4: Lawyer: who proved to be the neighbor?

A4: Jesus: the one who showed mercy.

Pope Francis (2020, pp. #63-76) used this parable to point our attention to those who today are assaulted, robbed, abused, and left in the ditches of life. He also highlighted the robbers we know and see all around us. Pope Francis underscored what Jesus told the lawyer, and us, to go and do likewise in caring for the needy even if they do not present as legally or religiously worthy as we might like.

Every client I saw over 40 years of practicing psychotherapy came into my office to tell me their story. The Bible is brimming with similar stories, and a highlight of those stories is the parables. Psychotherapy training includes case examples, and actual practice is a variety of responses to the stories of every client they see in their work. Thus, Jesus' stories can be unique demonstrations of interpersonal and spiritual competence and praxis for those seeking discernment skills.

The ACT movement has made great strides by including stories as an essential component of psychotherapy (Stoddard & Afari, 2014). From the ACT perspective, discernment is not simply figuring out complications of emotional-spiritual actions (1977, pp. 179-180), but requires informed clinical judgment in psychological, values, personality, and environmental terms.

Religious experience and discernment considerations lead to an imperative for CPA members to learn to "hear" clients' religious experiences. That is especially true for those far from religious practice or mired in mental health issues? Even if we are open to "hearing them," how will we exercise a combined clinically informed judgment and spiritual discernment?

It is a work of a lifetime for any of us to combine clinical judgment and religious/spiritual discernment. However, now is a good time, a graced time to begin.

Pope Francis has been named the discernment pope (Austin, 2018). As a Jesuit, he is undoubtedly aware of St. Ignatius Loyola's writings on discernment. However, he aims to expand and focus our range and focus of convenience, including the individual's dealing with emotional and spiritual states in our discernment of the context of the poor, those seeking justice, and his hope for the church (Ivereigh, 2018). Thus, ACT is a model that can augment more theological approaches to discernment.

In my years of practicing psychotherapy, I used many ACT workbooks and leaned toward the ACT approaches because they worked! ACT is rooted in the CBT (cognitive behavioral therapy) tradition but also represents a current cutting-edge approach to psychotherapy. For now, I find ACT includes some of the best we therapists have.

Like Pope Francis, ACT operates out of a philosophy called contextualism (Hayes S. , Functional Contextualism) in which psychological events interact in and with situationally defined contexts. We may be able to conceptually define and separate elements, but they are ontologically a whole. Their common goal is to avoid conforming blindly to social expectations. In theological terms, the goal is to "be transformed by the renewal of your mind, so that you may judge what is God's will, what is good, pleasing, and perfect" (Romans 12:1-2).

Our stories and reflecting on our stories to later share them can be emotionally and cognitively strenuous. After sharing one of my stories, I feel a sense of release, empowerment, and insight. However, I also feel naked before my readers.

Still, we need to reflect on our stories to move toward discernment and enter artistically into the biblical-Wisdom stories. To do that, we have to get personal! That means not letting modesty stop us, or fear, or embarrassment

In her poem *Sometimes*, the poet, Mary Oliver, put this issue of entering into the narrative style:

Instructions for living a life:

Pay attention.
Be astonished.
Tell about it.

Jesus spoke prophetically in words that were disorienting, amazing, and then reorienting. Namely, he proclaimed (Luke 12:2-3) that what we have heard in the secret of our hearts will all be made known in time, and what we have whispered behind closed doors will be proclaimed from the rooftops.

The only choice we have in this is whether we will leave it *for another to proclaim what God has revealed to us in secret prayer* to the benefit of all the tired, fed-up, and disillusioned of the world or *if we will dare to witness to the Spirit in our voices*. It's our choice.

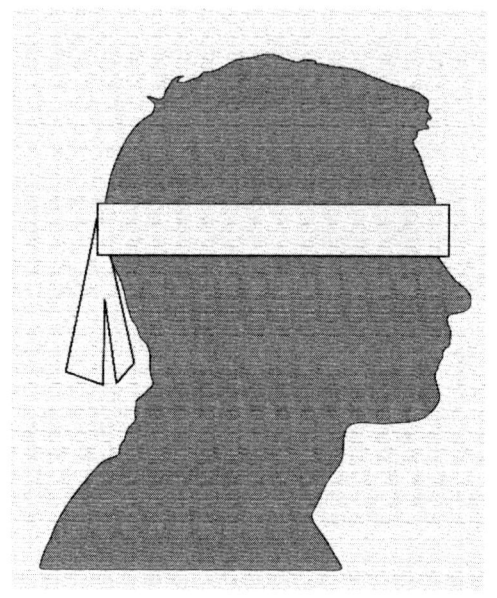

Figure 3

Our blindness.

James Jasper

3

WISDOM OUT OF BLINDNESS

Our blindness both spiritual and psychological is hidden from us. We hope that Jesus pledged that his followers who listened to his parables would receive insight that enlightens their spiritual blindness. Likewise, ACT works to relieve psychological blindness.

For example, in the Bible, Peter, James, and John perceived the Holy Spirit's presence as an overshadowing cloud on the mount of transfiguration. The three fell on their faces within the cloud. In the same way, the Spirit's presence is so outside our usual range of experience that we perceive God's presence and action as darkness to our minds.

In psychotherapy, clients likewise routinely experience symptoms, but the thinking, feeling, and acting patterns that contribute to the symptoms are outside their awareness as treatment begins. However, it hopefully enters their awareness as treatment continues.

Unless we remove our blindfolds, our lack of understanding can distort our perceptions of others and make interpersonal communication difficult or nearly impossible. Until we are open to removing our perceptual blindfolds, we limit our ability to hear Jesus' words, empathize with others, and, as therapists, help others observe their own inner and outer world experiences more objectively.

The biblical story that applies here is Jesus' use of two comparisons to demonstrate the need to know ourselves before guiding or doing psychotherapy with others. In two short parables (Luke 6:37-42), he gave two concrete **examples of spiritual blindness**, **"**Can a blind person guide a blind person? Will not both fall into a pit?" and "Why do you notice the splinter in your brother's eye, but do not perceive the wooden beam in your own?"

Jesus identified our spiritual blindness as the fundamental obstacle to effective interactions with others. For example, those blind spots may include a personal failure or past hurt that can make us defensive. Or failure to forgive some slight might manifest as subtle resentments or feelings of hopelessness. Jesus' point is that our inability to seek forgiveness for our hidden faults or even recognize them is like a wooden beam from the lumber yard, they blind us to our behavior.

ACT describes these blind spots as some combination of remaining stuck in the past, half-hearted commitment in the measure of our care and concern for others, or as disconnects between our stated values and how we apply them. Unless we attend to them, when we approach God, we may receive "the measure with which we measured others" as an answer to our prayers we would prefer not to receive.

To put this in a different frame of reference, we must make judgments all day long about things: whether it is safe to cross the street, what to eat for breakfast, and so on. However, we encounter the great unknowns or the barely knowable when reflecting on the nature of God, others, and self. Removing our personal "blindfolds is essential to three tasks. First, it is essential for the discernment of God's will. Second, removal of our blind spots is essential if we are to correctly recognize the perceptions of others. Third, hard work, courage, and insight are essential if we are to recognize our personal biases and conflicted motivations.

This parable and discernment are, in context, that CPA members train to sort through mental health aspects of a client's life that are intimately intertwined with any expression of religious experiences. In the earlier book, I offered a few initial criteria for determining the validity of religious/spiritual experiences. I also mentioned some of the theologians and psychologists who have asserted that religious experiences are universal and too often ignored or distorted.

The previous book advocated for not ignoring them, but second-level issues remain, namely, how must psychotherapists sort through the pervasive distortions in those same religious experiences? Religious experiences without discernment are a recipe for a mess! Even writing about the wisdom of insight is a daunting task. The biblical author, N.T. Wright said that any attempt to speak or write about the Bible is like building sandcastles before the Matterhorn Mountain. But let's try anyway.

In the simplest dictionary definition, discernment is the ability to judge well. However, judging well depends on the person's starting point. If the person is a delivery person, it may mean finding the best route and managing the time and distance between drop-off points. For a structural engineer designing a new bridge, accurately perceiving the stress points, and using the appropriate formula to predict the characteristics of the requisite steel beams would be a much more complex discernment. Sound judgment and best practice might be exponentially difficult for an emergency medicine physician.

As a result of humanity's blindness to God, others, and self, it is challenging for us to develop what ACT calls "a sense of self" that can step back and observe our current experiences as more than our immediate thoughts, feelings, and actions.

Perceptual bias toward God, others, and self are evident in countless personal issues, patterns in government, dimmed awareness of our effects on our earth's environment, the horrors of war, and countless more.

I dare to offer one example. Namely, the United States sustained approximately 3,000 casualties on 9/11. Our country responded with a mixture of national pride, partial blindness to the effects on others, and a blossoming of fear. Our response included heightened travel security at home and the invasion of two countries, Iraq and Afghanistan. We spent at least $2 trillion on that response. Brown University (Watson Institute of International & Public Affairs of Brown University, 2021) tabulated over 801,000 civilian casualties. Kagan (2021), a historian, argues that our 9/11 security decisions are still disrupting many parts of the world and are one factor in our current struggle to preserve our democracy. In short, we are still far from able to digest our national history or even the history of the past two decades.

Rather than struggle with the present, it is perhaps easier to be objective about the past. An example from past battles, disruption, conflicted goals, and distorted intentions are the experiences of a prophetic laywoman, St. Joan of Arc.

Joan was burned at the stake in 1431 at age 19. Mark Twain wrote a most exceptional biography of her. He said of his other books that they required no preparation and got none. However, Twain reported spending 14 happy years deciphering the Inquisition's hand-written transcripts of her trial. The theology department at Oxford prepared three English versions, and the theology department at the University of Paris prepared three French versions. The duplicate copies were each a word-for-word transcript of her defense before the inquisition. Day after day, she was brought from her cell and seated in a chair on a raised witness platform. Then, daily, this unlettered young woman bested the theologians of the Universities of Paris and Oxford, two of the best theology schools that time had to offer. If it were tennis, we would say she won every set. If she lost a set, she would die.

Within 20 years after her death, she was rehabilitated with high-ranking political and religious leaders admitting the errors in judgment and the blindness of the time that led to her death. However, it took centuries for France to recognize her not just as a revolutionary figure but as a holy person.

Mark Twain had a role in that recognition. After several attempts that didn't come together, Twain (1835, 1910) sorted and arranged the transcripts plus the memoirs of her life-long friend and companion into a readable story.

There is nothing left of her. The soldiers at her execution burned her remains three times over so no shred of her would remain. During the turmoil of French 19th century, zealots destroyed her few remaining artifacts: a banner and a couple of personal items.

In celebrating the 500th anniversary of France, Joan was "rediscovered" as someone who had been present at the beginning of the national state. France reportedly pressed the Vatican for her canonization and in 1920 Pope Benedict XV declared her a saint. She is a saint-martyr canonized based on her sworn testimony.

Hopefully, it will not take the United States the 500 years it took France in St. Joan's case to appreciate her merit and moderate their national blindness.

The cost of discernment comes into focus in Jesus' parable of the **tower builder** (Luke 14:28-30) calculating the cost of construction before beginning. His words, "Which one of you?" warned each of us seeking spiritual perfection that we must first calculate the cost of learning wisdom and discernment and then take the additional step of putting those words into practice (Snodgrass, 2018, pp. 379-388). His parables about the tower builder or **the king going to war** (Luke 14:31-32) are parables of challenge and warning. Together, the two parables prioritized God's discernment over all the world's wisdom and values (Wenham, 1989, pp. 203-204).

In separating himself from the terms and values of his age, Jesus followed in the wisdom path of distinguishing his discipleship from the practices of any other age or system. The early Christians had to stand back from Greek wisdom and insist that Biblical wisdom began with fear of the Lord (Wablen, 2008, p. 846).

Our task today is to distinguish Jesus' discipleship from other value systems.

Jesus warned his disciples (Blomberg, 2012, pp. 385-390) of the consequences of choosing to become his disciple. Though learning from Jesus meant freedom from fears of pain and discomfort. Such a life also included personal crosses to carry, the possible loss of all property (the tower parable), or even death (the king going to battle parable). Jesus urged that we not even begin to travel with him if we have not seriously considered the consequences (cf. 2 Peter 2:21).

Blomberg (p. 388) added that transformation with Jesus takes time. Over time, carrying our crosses (Luke 14:27) involves more than mouthing platitudes or professing belief without taking committed action (p. 390).

Jesus' warnings are anti-marketing in their approach and the opposite of the prosperity gospel. He also warned against the health and wealth gospel, the approach to faith that donations to religious causes will increase one's material wealth. Instead, Jesus stressed that to follow him, we need to renounce all our possessions (Luke 14:25-32) and trust that God will provide all we need rather than all we want or desire. That is a tall order.

To follow Jesus even means prioritizing the needs of the Gospel over family ties (Luke 14:26). That does not mean avoiding family needs but trusting that even family is healthier if God is first in the family.

Our stories suffer the assaults of daily news feeds that reinforce our blind spots. Thus, we pray that God's Holy Spirit will deliver us from our blindness and unveil our vision of ourselves, of our world, and of God.

To develop our discernment skills, I advocate that before we evaluate either biblical stories or our clients' stories, we first reflect on our stories. Effortful cognitive exercises such as reflecting on our life are beneficial discernment skills because of their effect on our brain physiology and cognition (Hankle, 2013, p. 25). With that in mind, I invite you to reflect on your story as a profound experience. However, I must warn you that while I have found it both personally and professionally beneficial, it has been hard work overcoming my embarrassment, acknowledging my shortcomings, and sharing my inner world.

You can find an outline for reflecting on your story in worksheet #2, Telling Our Stories.

Possibilities are lurking within our stories. Our stories, including Jesus' parables and other biblical stories, are part of the antidote for 500 years of the historical drift toward skepticism, cynicism, materialism, and boredom.

Remember that stories can link our thoughts with our feelings and actions, so as you reflect on your account, identify each statement as a thought, a feeling, or an action. See worksheet #3, About Thinking, Feeling, and Acting (T-F-A).

Focusing on an incident in your life,

    a.   What was good about it?

    b.   What was bad about it?

    c.   How was God present for you in it?

In the index of my book on religious experience (Biersbach, 2021) I included an index with many personal examples. If you have trouble beginning to focus on God's action in your life you might try reading some of that index. However, that's my story. What about prayerfully searching through your story and begging the Holy Spirit to show you what was important, what your struggles were, and where God was for you?

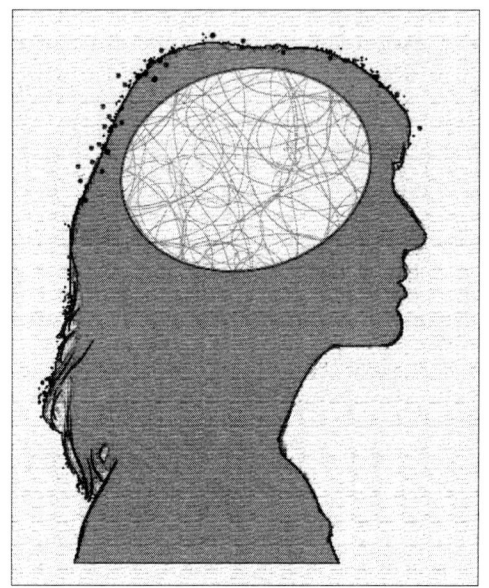

Figure 4

Our need for discernment.

James Jasper

4

DISCERNMENT: AN ONGOING TASK

Three mindsets in the parables can convince us that discernment is not one-and-done. It is a life-long task to sort all we see and hear as we perceive God's will for us in each moment and strive to serve our clients wisely.

With that in mind, let us search a bit more for help and guideposts in the ongoing task of knowing and living the will of God versus our own will. As the saying goes, we either say to God, "Your will be done," or God says to us, "Your will be done!"

Bear in mind that the parables do not exist to confirm our presuppositions and biases, nor do Jesus' stories exist to reinforce our blindness. Rather, if we attend to them, the parables prod and encourage us toward beginning the process of shaping our assumptions and relieving our impaired vision.

For starters, do we accept that grappling with Jesus' stories is an essential first step in the T-F-A (thinking-feeling-acting) transformation process as psychotherapists? How do we present to clients that reexamining our T-F-A is an essential step in transforming psychological dead-ends and spiritual blindness?

The biblical parable of the father of the profligate and the resentful sons (Luke 15:11–32) illustrates three characters but also the mindsets of the three characters.

As Blomberg (2012, pp. 200-201) wrote, Jesus' intent in this parable was that, like the prodigal, we always have the option of repenting and returning home to our heavenly Father, if we admit our shortcomings and turn to God in repentance, as did the younger son. The parable highlights the lengths God our Father goes to offer reconciliation to all people. The Father lavished forgiveness and restoration of dignity on his younger son as symbolized by the signet ring and the robe. Conversely, God urged the elder brother to rejoice in the brother's return rather than resent it.

Though this parable is about two sons, it is also about all of God's children. The forgiving father, the story suggests, had looked for his child many times. Even though his younger child had squandered his birthright wastefully, the father welcomed the wandering son's repentant return. The loving father also pleaded with his resentful elder son, who nurtured fantasies of his younger brother's sexual acting out and begrudged the younger son's forgiveness. Sadly, at the end of the parable, the older brother remained resentful for his father not praising and celebrating his hard work.

Discernment and this parable's underlying meaning are veiled from some because of their mindsets and perspectives from "seeing." Such blindness might include a rationale based on one of the following perspectives:

a. Biology: that we are biologically predisposed to develop the attitudes and behaviors we exhibit (Hibbing, Smith, & Alford, 2014) so we are the victims of our biology.

b. Sociology: Haidt (2012) characterized the younger son as a liberal (Trueman, 2020) and the elder a conservative (Francis, 2021) so our blindness is the result of our political inclinations.

c. Family systems: such conflicts are simply sibling rivalry and are simply the way of things.

d. Finance: financial advisors might characterize the younger son as a poor investor or consumer of goods, while the elder was wise to preserve the family estate and to defer consumption in favor of savings. In this perspective, it is financial pressures that shape our mindsets.

e. The Law: in demanding his share of the inheritance, the younger brother acted selfishly and insensitively but was legally correct so here legal rights and obligations influence our points of view.

f. Popular sentiment: based on polls and other research Edsall (2021) argued that radical differences between, for example, liberals and conservatives depend on education level, the basis of personal identity, and acceptance or refusal to empathize and listen to the perspective of the other. Each side believes that their position is the moral one, and each hopes to name the essential issue of the other in simplistic terms (Brooks, 2021). This malignant mindset judges others from rigid stereotypes.

g. Psychology: the behavior of the brothers is due to personality factors (Gurven, Rueden, Massenkoff, Kaplan, & Vie, 2012) or personality types and the pattern's enduring patterns of thinking, feeling, and acting. The younger son's behavior was exploitive toward his father and irresponsible in using money so we might label him a mixture of narcissistic or antisocial. The elder son was resentful, contrary, skeptical, and disappointed. He entertained fantasies of his brother's time with prostitutes though his brother did not mention sex with prostitutes. The elder brother sounds like a negativistic personality (Millon & Davis, 1996, p. 139), displacing his fantasies onto his brother. In this view, our attitudes are the result of personality traits or disorders.

How can we acknowledge that each of these perspectives has some truth yet square those perspectives with the parable?

If we are to "learn to discern" and become good guides in psychotherapy we can wonder who is the best at living as an authentic Christian? We can wonder how we can find certainty.

Dubay wrote a book on such certitude. Further, in 1977 he wrote a book on discernment (1977) that clarifies the confusion over the words to describe the discernment processes, and how authentic experiences can and should be validated externally and internally. Fr. Dubay, who died in 2010, appears to have been a terrific person, priest, and writer. However, he said not a word that I can find connecting discernment with psychology or psychotherapy. So, be aware that I look to the great doctors of the church as well as spiritual writers such as him, but I also include psychotherapeutic resources. That combining of resources is consistent with the vision of the Catholic Psychotherapy Association (CPA).

For starters, we can acknowledge that our bent perceptions move us to act on our own will more frequently than we should. At least I do despite my best efforts. "Cashing in" our future options and opportunities to act out some desire motivated by some distorted self-talk creeps into my consciousness like weeds into our family garden. At other times I overtly act justly but my fantasies seethe with some resentment, criticize the acting out of others, or begrudge the fun and reward others are enjoying. In contrast, I am the "good one" who lacks those advantages. It is only in daily prayer that I can weed all these out of my consciousness.

Is that process familiar to you as well? Do you occasionally waver between the pattern of the older and younger brother? Conversely, do you find that over time, an effect of growing in virtue is that the range of those swings becomes less and less?

ACT urges both sides, the acting out and the resentful, to develop a critical psychological factor: flexibility of response. As Edsall (2021) put it,

> Individuals who are cognitively inflexible and intolerant of ambiguity may become captive audiences for ideological, political, or religious extremists whose simplistic worldviews gloss over nuance. Indeed, cognitive inflexibility has been positively associated with authoritarian aggression, racism, and ethnocentrism.

That is, the ACT approach to psychotherapy aims to increase flexibility in adaptation to many psychological problem areas rather than taking sides as if the issue is either-or.

As the prodigal son story concluded, we have no idea what happened to the characters. How did the prodigal and resentful sons act, think, and feel the next day?

How did the younger son cope the next day with life at home? Behaviorally, he had returned home, but how did he work through his past guilt on squandering his share of the family estate? Did he and his brother get into an argument the following day with the younger blaming the older for being a cheapskate (financial) who had always looked down on him (family systems)? Did the younger start working and doing his share or mope around the house (values)? Did he boast to his brother that at least he had said he was sorry, but his brother liked to rub it in how the younger had messed up (personality)?

As for the older son, he was unrepentant when last we saw him. Did he judge his brother a chronic loser by nature (biology) or think of him as a libertine willing to distort the intent of the law (legal) if given half a chance (sociology)? Did the elder listen to his friends who agreed that his father should never have taken him back without further repentance (forgiveness process)?

Thus, excellent as the parable's description of the beginnings of repentance in the younger son, the hard-heartedness of the elder son, and the extent of the loving father's forgiveness and concern, each brother remained free to live the next day on their terms or the father's. The father figure, like God, does not force them or us to choose the way of wisdom or to live by our own rules. All the forces I listed: biology, legal, financial, social, personality, family systems, psychological, and probably many more constantly remain in play.

In a hopeful development, the ACT approach (Hayes S. , ACT Therapeutic Steps) proposes several psychotherapeutic steps that can conceivably assist in the more theological process of forgiveness and transformation. Namely, Hayes listed nine strategies for approaching personal and client change.

1. Compassionately confront the unworkable agenda, always appealing to the client's experience as the ultimate arbiter.

2. Help clients find a place from which they can admit their T-F-A, that is, what they are feeling, think, and doing.

3. In the service of that goal, teach acceptance and defusion skills.

4. Help the client make richer and less defended contact with the present moment and their ongoing thoughts, feelings, and sensations.

5. Help the client encounter a transcendent sense of self.

6. Help the client become more consistently mindful.

7. Help the client move in a direction consistent with their professed values.

8. Help the client detect traps, fusions, and strange loops as defined in the ACT literature.

9. Repeat, and expand the scope of the work. Then, keep repeating and expanding the steps until the clients generalize, that is, say in some broad way what they have deduced from their repeated negative habits.

If the strategies are perplexing for you, think about finding some ACT reading or training. However, take heart because, in my experience, the ACT interventions "work," and a growing body of empirical research supports it. Hopefully, my comments will pique your interest in learning more about ACT.

Our stories contain the footprints of our daily habits and blinding patterns. To counter them St. Benedict held that the purpose of monastic life was a daily inner conversation with self about our habits of life and reflecting on and doing a "U-turn" as necessary to become living saints. Swoboda (2018) offers an extended reflection on courageous change.

Did the parable of the two sons influence you? Do you have an account of your resolution to prioritize daily change? How did your resolution work for you?

Remember that stories can link heaven and earth. Part of what makes realistic stories so impressive is that such stories feature at least one person speaking in the first person. Try speaking in the first person in your story. Is there a moment that comes to mind that illustrates how God has worked with your strengths, your weaknesses in crucial moments or provided what you needed in that time?

    a. What was good about it?

    b. What was bad about it?

    c. How was God present for you in it?

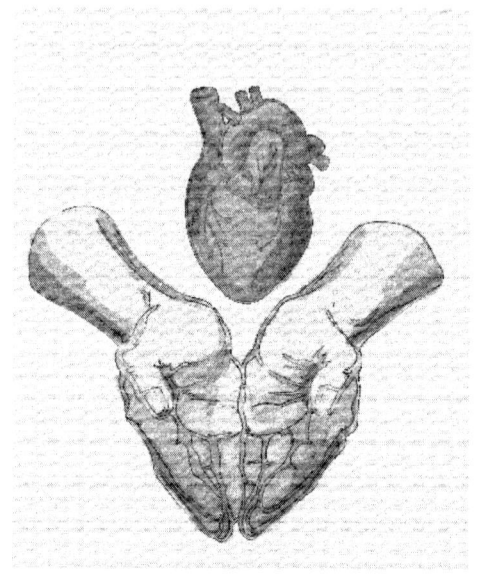

Figure 5

Parables open the human heart

James Jasper

5

WHY PARABLES?

Stories that unveil human hearts are an operational definition of the effectiveness of parables.

Parables are tools to compare something physical to something spiritual. Jesus began several parables by saying, "The Kingdom of God is like." Thus, he tied an abstract concept (the Kingdom of God) to something more concrete and visible (Halloran, 2013).

Along with parables, storytellers use yarns of all types to 1) provide a context, 2) isolate factors the storyteller considers essential, and 3) show all the parts of the story—beginning, middle, end—in one suspenseful narrative. For example, in creative writing professors stress that effective stories lead up to one or more dramatic points (Gillispie, 2003). An example of such dramatic points is the vast popularity of football as a metaphor for life (Clarke, 2009).

Storytellers aim to lead their hearers to new perspectives that, at first glance, depending on our starting point, might not fit with their set perspectives or assumptions.

Thus, Jesus taught with parables for two primary purposes 1) to explain the truth to some and 2) to keep truths hidden from others (Halloran, 2013). In popular terms, we might say that raconteurs construct jokes so that some will "get it" and others won't. Parables were memorable illustrations of a kingdom principle for those eager to follow God. For those opposed to God's plans, the meaning of the parables is an unperceived judgment where the resistant listeners do not perceive the verdict.

The focus here is the parables because they are a large part of Jesus' preaching. They are about a third of his recorded teaching. They are stories unique in the literature of the world. They are brief and articulate, and they appear mundane and straight-forward at first glance. However, upon revisit, they prove to be anything but simple.

Because the parables are stories, they draw us in and, for a moment, exclude all else. Jesus' stories tug at us even when we "get" them only superficially. Despite our dullness, we cannot make them into what we want. Or perhaps we strive to make the parable elements fit piece by piece into our current situations. Instead, the parables force us to reflect on what Jesus' intent was as he told the tale. Yet embedded in their own time as Jesus' stories were, they somehow simultaneously illuminate God's intrusion into moments in our time as well.

The sayings of Jesus contain a tremendous amount of teaching in visible and active form. Plus, parables intend to unveil the hardened heart. In that, their intent is remarkably similar to the psychotherapeutic task of diminishing dullness, accepting life as it is, and then committing to transformation in therapy and life.

Some scholars expend their energies demonstrating that the parables are not analogies. However, Jesus' interpreted parables such as the three in Matthew chapter 13—the sower and the seed, the weeds in the grain, and the net—are expanded analogies, that is, a series of related metaphors (Snodgrass, 2018, p. 2).

A similar dead-end can be getting caught up in endless debates on how many parables there are. Instead, I advocate for simply accepting that the biblical stores can include similes, metaphors, parables, analogies, and what Jeremias calls parabolic actions (1963, pp. 227-229). The example Jeremias gave was Jesus welcoming and embracing little children as models of the poor in spirit.

The biblical stories are not just figures of speech, but a uniquely consistent way of thinking that is experiential, timeless, and requires no previous training to understand. I find it remarkable that though the script of the parables is the same for everyone, even the great scholars project into them elements consistent with their unique point of view. The result is an enormous range of categorizing, numbering, and interpreting the parables.

Regardless of where a reader stands on these debates, there's nothing quite like Jesus' parables. They remain jewels, masterpieces, able to hide and reveal. Jesus chose to teach in story form because stories engage the mind and emotions of listeners like no other form of teaching.

A biblical story that applies here is that when alone with him, Jesus' disciples asked, as we might, **why he spoke to them and still speaks to us in parables** (Mark 4:10-12). He replied that his paradoxical stories have a unique quality. That is, those who follow him were enabled to learn from them facets of the kingdom of God while those who rejected God and Jesus looked and saw but did not perceive, listened but failed to understand. The result was that God's word to them could not convert them so they could find forgiveness.

Blomberg's (2012, pp. 231-232) commentary on Jesus' statement of intent in telling parables (Mark 4:10-12) is that his statement demonstrates that first, God is patient and longsuffering in waiting for his people to bear the fruit he requires of them, even when they are repeatedly and overtly hostile in their rebellion against him.

Second, a day will come when God's patience is exhausted, and those who have rejected Him, He will banish from his presence. Then, God will accomplish his purposes in and through His stories because he will bring in new leaders who will produce the fruit the original listeners failed to provide.

Overall, **the purpose of parables** includes:

    a. Answering questions from critics

    b. Redirecting questioners to alternative perspectives

    c. Modeling virtue, discernment, flexibility, and context

d. Modeling connection to God, others, and creation

e. Piercing listener's veils of avoidance.

The discernment principle here is that Jesus' intended purpose in using parables is paradoxical. Their meaning is a seemingly absurd or self-contradictory statement or proposition that proves well-founded or true when investigated or explained.

If we look more closely at the parables, it is fair to ask what Jesus' paradoxical purpose might be. In answer, Blomberg (2012, p. 448) proposed three purposes in Jesus' use of stories, namely, the graciousness of God, the demands of discipleship and the dangers of disobedience.

Overall, the central theme uniting all the lessons of the parables is the kingdom of God. It is both present and future. It is the almighty power of God. That is, the parables are essential because we are so enmeshed in our prejudices, blindness, and social bonds that only stories that begin with some physical situation or social dilemma can introduce us to Jesus' mysterious salvation and deliverance goals.

Jesus intentionally started several parables by saying, "The Kingdom of God is like." His process is the three-step approach of the OT wisdom literature such as the psalms. Namely, the storyteller first focuses listeners on some concrete object or situation. Second, the narrator connects the object to a spiritual reality, and lastly, the chronicler leads listeners to an icon that becomes proverbial. For example, we can refer to a mustard seed or the prodigal son, and the values of those stories come to mind.

I use the word "stories" because scholarly efforts to distinguish parables from other figures of speech such as similes, analogies, and metaphors have been a complete failure (Snodgrass, 2018, p. 16). The problem is that Jesus moved seamlessly from one figure of speech to another. As a master storyteller, He used his stories to respond to questions put to Him. His stories expanded on the proclamation of God's intention to redeem us even when we are lost and unaware that we are lost. In Jesus, God comes to us as a shepherd sent to guide and protect us (e.g., Psalm 80:1, 95:7; John 10:11, 14).

Our stories are tools that can help us align with what's current today? Therefore, work on telling your story to yourself! Our stories are a way of knowing ourselves (Wilson, 2014).

As you dig into the deep riches of Christ's parables, consider

○ What influence does each of Jesus' parables have on me?

○ Does the parable or story in each chapter lead me to a more profound decision for God?

○ Am I moved to give an individual witness to those close to me?

The parables will help us listen anew and attentively in a childlike fashion to Jesus' word to us today. Working through the dynamics of each parable will hopefully allow us to accept unconditionally what each presents. The process of unveiling involves looking anew at our motivation and our understanding of God (Bock, 2012).

The paradox with Jesus' stories is that some things are problematic because they are complex while others appear simple, but their meaning escapes the listener. That is what Jesus meant in saying that to those "outside," everything comes in parables, so that those outsiders may look and see but not perceive, and hear and listen but not understand, so that they may not find conversion and forgiveness (Mark 4:12). Only those characterized by poverty of spirit can pierce that veiled meaning.

So, our reflection time is a chance to be alone with Jesus, to ask him questions, just as the apostles did. It is a chance to learn anew about the mysteries of the kingdom of God. It is also an opportunity (costs) to refocus on God's plan and perspective for us because, as Jesus promised, "The mystery of the kingdom of God has been granted to you."

It is a chance to beg the Spirit to unveil our blindness and bring us forgiveness and healing (John 12:40c). Consider again whether a specific instance or moment comes to mind that illustrates how God 1) has worked with your strengths and weaknesses, 2) been with you in crucial moments or 3) provided what you needed in that time?

    a. What was good about that moment or instance?

    b. What was bad about it?

    c. How was God present for you in it?

Figure 6

The growth of campfire communities in isolation

Chalk & Blade

6

WHY WE LIKE STORIES

Stories with their narrative styles can fit nicely our study of discernment. The premiere example of stories applied is the biblical wisdom tradition with its style and pattern that is quite distinct from the priestly and prophetic traditions.

Grant (2008, p. 861) stresses that it is unwise to draw too sharp a distinction between the wisdom tradition in the Bible and the other traditions. Instead, we might notice that Jesus compares the people of God to a fig tree. Thus, the tree's roots, trunk, and leaves must each do their part to be fruitful like the three traditions. See Worksheet #4, The Three Traditions in the worksheets section later in the book.

However, my task is to avoid too rigidly distinguishing the three traditions. Though the lifestyle of each has a customary path to follow in being faithful to the Gospel, they are interconnected, and each approach is necessary for the Church's life of faith. The three are more like a tree's roots, branches, and leaves, each essential if the tree thrives. Thus, today, we distinguish the overt lifestyles of parish priests, vowed religious living in community, and the laity, but each has an essential role.

What is significant is that the three traditions have distinct approaches to discernment. The literature on the priestly and prophetic perspectives on discernment is better known. However, the laity has a unique history, and its path is in development. That is, the role of the laity is emerging in new ways in our time. A crucial milestone was the Vatican II Decree on the Apostolate of the Laity (1975) that in 1965 pointed to aspirational goals for lay apostolates. However, the steps to proceed on the secular path require development.

As the Genesis account put it, it is not easy to struggle alone with our inner world. Because of that, stories help meet the human need to share our inner world with others by naming our inner world to allow others to become partners in our life journeys. That is true for both psychological and religious experiences.

Storytellers construct their tales by selecting some elements as significant and omitting others. In listening to stories that "grab us," the storyteller says that the story's priorities, highlights, and essential elements give meaning and zest to life.

To return to the theme of the three biblical traditions, the language of the Wisdom literature was storytelling through music, novellas, artful writing, theatrical drama, wise sayings, and shared experiential moments. These are all means to resolve the spiritual/secular, material/spiritual dichotomy. The Wisdom books' authors fused God and creation. The authors used stylistic forms, for example, in Job, a dramatic poem, and in the short novels.

The Catechism (United States Catholic Conference, 1995, p. #546) says that Jesus' parables present us with a decision to choose for or against the good described in each story. That forced-choice parallels clients' psychotherapy stories in that both types of stories necessitate a turn toward or away from psychological and spiritual well-being.

Biblical stories capture and celebrate the cultures in which Jesus' parables occurred, but their images and metaphors can have rich meanings to those living in the 21st century.

Discernment in biblical stories and parables is like clients' stories in that **not** every minor detail has a significant meaning. Because parables are stories, they sometimes need supporting information for the main idea of the parable to make sense and have its power.

Emotions can powerfully twist what we consider clear plans toward ineffective and inefficient decisions (Hankle, 2013, p. 22). That is, when emotions arise, they can lead us to incorrect conclusions. But when authors place emotions within parables and stories, the initial and ongoing influences that produce feelings become more apparent. Also, stories leave final decisions for the hearer to work out without the pressures those living the events might experience. That is, stories are platforms for learning to handle emotions better.

The beauty and art of the wisdom books have evidential value (Dubay, 1999) because when we read or hear their narratives, the artful lyrical beauty draws us in.

As humanity discovered, sitting around campfires and telling artful stories captured the emotions and imaginations of listeners. It was storytelling as an art form. A remarkable amount of research on the charred remains of human fires supports the theories that our ancestors began to interact with and control fire over a space of a million years (Burton, 2011). With fire, humans found warmth, lighting, pushback against predators, and a way to cook food.

Pollan (2013) pointed out that we are the only animal that cooks. With cooking, humans could eat soft food and reduce the 50% of their time most animals spend chewing. Over time we humans developed smaller jaws that made speech possible. Plus, our heads had room for larger brains with smaller jaws, and with bigger brains, weapons for hunting followed.

There were also painfully gradual social effects over epic periods evidenced by remarkable anthropological studies of charred fuel and remnants of bone (Burton, 2011). Evidence shows that humans hunted and cooked in small groups. Fed and warmed, they gathered to share meaning through stories in the darkness. Early humans could pass on current hunting information and remembered history through storytelling. The campfire became an island of safety that fostered food sharing and language development. Their stories were a way to make sense of their world by identifying heroes and villains.

Stories connect inner and outer motives with visible actions. Pollan (2013) casts Homer's epic as stories shared around cooked meals. Likewise, the Yahwist's (Ellis, 1968, pp. 21-30) theological history of Israel in Genesis chapters 2 to 11 originated as a series of stories passed down for generations among believers around campfires.

Long (2018, pp. 2-3) pointed out that Greek philosophy began with narratives reflecting on the nature of stability and change. Namely, an observer can see a river as a constant reality while the water flows and changes moment to moment. The traditional philosophical starting point for Aristotle in reflecting on change (the water) versus stability (the river) was being. Ontology, also called metaphysics, was the foundation of Greek philosophy, and the starting point was to ask what the nature was of being. All conclusions grew out of inferential philosophizing through analogy, induction, or deduction. The limiting factor on that problem is "the regress problem," in that all truth starts from previous inferences. Put bluntly, the approach scarcely touches the ground, and it is all beliefs based on other assumptions.

By comparison, **Genesis (2:18-24)** provides both a biblical methodology that unlocks human hearts and a process for unraveling both storytelling and psychotherapy.

That is, just as with Adam, our human intellectual task includes naming the world. We do that to organize reality mentally and make human sense of God's creation. God

> brought them to the man to see what he would call them; whatever the man called each of them would be its name. The man gave names to all the cattle, birds of the air, and wild animals, but none proved to be the suitable partner for the man (Gen. 2:19a).

This human task, the scientific task in theology, psychology, psychotherapy, and, in fact, in all the sciences, is to name the world, to categorize the world so that we can deal with the immensity of God's creation in bite-sized pieces.

If we talk about parables (Strawn, 2008) as stories, Genesis' chapters 1-11 are a string of narratives. The New American Bible (2012, p. 7) says succinctly that the twelve tribes had an oral form of their story from creation to taking the Promised Land.

That means that the Genesis stories, written down about 500 B.C., had been discussed for at least a thousand years. The earliest believers reflected on their faith and expressed that belief in the Genesis stories. Those countless believers did theology through storytelling before there were any theological terms besides stories.

The Church affirms that inspiration consisted of selecting some elements rather than others in those early ages. That reflection widened from representations of family, then clan, and tribe, and finally, the Israelite nation's growing awareness of their faith. The oral tradition did not end with Abraham, undoubtedly the first historical figure. Instead, that oral tradition continues today in the buzz of the People of God as we reflect on our faith.

Three lines from Genesis give us clues to the process.

First, the Bible says of humanity is that it is not good for humans to be alone. We do not do well alone. That is evident in individual therapy, where all our fears, hopes, disappointments, and inner conflicts emerge. In prison, solitary confinement is so damaging that a United Kingdom study found that even the most dangerous prisoners are confined in small pods where limited socialization with other dangerous prisoners is less harmful than total isolation (Salov, 2008). The point for us is that discernment is about those thoughts, reflections, and emotions that arise when we are alone at the most basic level. In contemporary psychotherapy, countless clients find themselves alone with their hopes, fears, losses, wounds, and the whole of their life stories.

Second, the words "whatever the man called each of them would be its name." The task assigned to the human was to name the animals. That task continues to this day in the behavioral science's mission to name clients' inner world so that we can make sense of our inner landscape and the processes that move that inner world. It is a vast and ongoing process.

Third, "none proved to be the suitable partner for the man." Genesis used the image of Eve made from a rib of Adam to graphically emphasize that there are the closest of links between the men and women.

Humanity's search for meaningful companions still consumes a large part of humanity's attention. Psychotherapy is intentionally a unique and specific kind of meaningful companionship, and it is a specialized kind of friendship.

The focus on friendship and connection is an alternative philosophical starting point. The result can be a philosophy focused on living rather than being (Long, 2018).

The result is a psychologically dynamic and biblically rich starting place. Thus, the foundation is not just to exist here or later in heaven or hell, but to LIVE and see God in the land of the living, for example, Psalm 142:5, Deuteronomy 10:8-9, Numbers 18:20, Psalm 119:57, Psalm 73:25-26, Job 20:29; 27:13; Ecclesiastes 9:9, plus all the New Testament references to new life and resurrection. While both approaches have their advantages, "living" is a theological starting point more congruent with the lively language of the biblical wisdom tradition than the more cognitive focus on being.

The functional-contextual perspective is a secular philosophy that parallels the Wisdom literature of the Bible. Rather than building a structure of hypotheses based on other assumptions, the contemporary contextualist perspective aims to connect philosophical data points with observable behavior. William James accomplished that in his *Varieties of Religious Experience*.

The ACT (Acceptance and Commitment Therapy) research is extensive and growing (ACBS: Association for Contextual Behavioral Science, n.d.). From ACT has come renewed cognitive-behavioral applications for psychotherapy that are remarkably like the perspective of the wisdom tradition. Thus, I hope CPA might foster psychotherapy and faith that are validated empirically following the functional contextualism paradigm (Long, p. 3-4). The wisdom tradition and ACT support linking inferences about people based on experience and interaction with the world and linking ACT and story narratives to connect life and psychotherapy.

This interaction with experience and with the world is called contextualism. Linking that experience through observable data points is functionalism, such as functional assessments in the DSM-5. The functional-contextual approach validates and anchors truth with human experience combines the two methodologies. It is admittedly messier and less ethereal than starting with being. However, the payoff makes both faith and psychotherapy more personally meaningful.

Our stories continue to merit our reflection and sharing as we pursue discernment based on unveiling our blindness.

In that effort, a helpful tip can be to remember that too many extraneous details can derail the whole point of our stories.

Have you ever composed a story to share at an open fire or fireplace or for sharing over food? Do you remember what those occasions might have been? In your storytelling,

a. What was good about it?

b. What was bad about it?

c. How was God present for you in it?

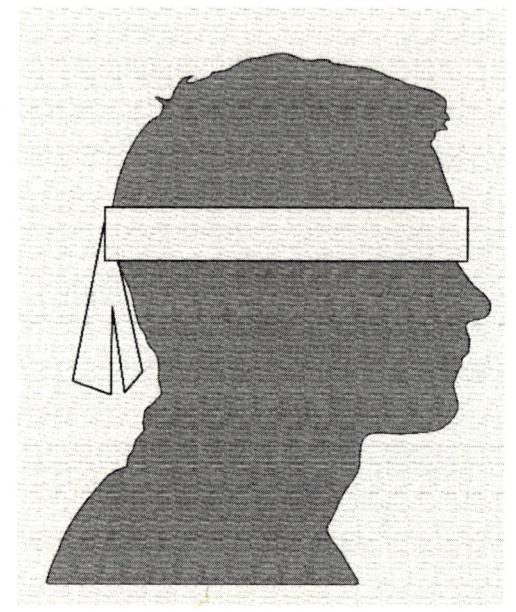

Figure 7

Kinds of blindness

James Jasper

7

DOING GOD'S WILL OR OURS

Unveiled eyes are what is Jesus trying to save us from in his stories. The psalms give us clues in understanding Jesus' intent. For example, consider one verse from the psalms (27:1), "The Lord is my light and my salvation; whom should I fear? The Lord is my life's refuge; of whom should I be afraid?"

That perspective of filling our hearts with light and assuaging our fears implies that without God's help, our darkness and fear veil our perceptions. That is the sense of Jesus saying that whoever does not accept the kingdom of God like a child will not enter it.

As a sign of your childlikeness, I invite you to reflect on your life. Much of what you read here will fall into place if you can do that because the kingdom of God belongs to those childlike in their defenselessness toward love.

A biblical image for this paradox is that the parables are veiled. This pattern of providing images even for veiled hearts is characteristic of the wisdom literature's three-step process of starting with concrete objects, then adding a spiritual component, and finally the development of an icon-image that supports prayer, worship, and joy (Strawn, 2008, p. 310)

The parable that applies here is the story of the **two debtors** (Luke 7:41-43) is a juridical parable (Snodgrass, 2018, pp. 77-91). That is, it asks who shall inherit the family property. Instead, Jesus deflected and reoriented the initial question with "What is your opinion?" and thereby turned the issue to who shall inherit the kingdom of God.

Note, this story is bracketed conceptually by the parables of the two builders (Luke 6:46-49) and the Sower and the seed (Luke 9:1-6). In each tale, Jesus compared the obstinate or unrepentant to the wise and faithful. He took his fellow dinner guests to task by unfavorably comparing the hosts to the sinful woman (Luke 7:44-50).

The parable's purpose is clear. God requires sincere repentance, not just the appearance of social acceptance. Jesus' intent is even more apparent if we keep in mind the parable of **the two sons** (Matthew 21:28-32). Participation in religious practices, such as going to church and being "yes-sayers," is insufficient (Snodgrass, 2018, pp. 266-275). It is even preferable to begin wicked and seek repentance as the sinful woman did in the two-debtors example than to become visibly faithful but internally only socially compliant.

Both parables focus on decision and indecision. <u>Being indecisive or ambivalent blinds us and keeps us from moving forward in mental health and spiritual life.</u> The Bible refers to this ambivalence with several terms. However, one biblical image I think is appropriate here is "hardness of heart" as a veiled or blindfolded heart.

Rather than saying, "unveil your hearts," Jesus modeled a similar behavior by unconditionally accepting the woman's beautiful repentance with ointment and tears that illustrated the opposite of hard-heartedness. Jesus' unwavering acceptance of the manner of the woman's repentance was so openhearted that his behavior embarrassed his fellow diners.

A similar reaction from a crowd was that after Moses returned from meeting God, his face shone (Ex. 34:29), which frightened all who saw him (v. 31).

A practice with a long history that still endures is that many brides still cover their faces at weddings. Historically, we can look back to about 1850 BC when Rachel covered her face when she first saw Isaac but undoubtedly uncovered it later that day after their wedding (Gen. 24:65). A wedding veil is a conscious sign of a bride's intention to unveil her inner life to her beloved.

When I did psychotherapy with couples, if I caught a glimpse of what I call their secret intimate smile, I suspected they'd make it as a couple.

Discernment through stories leads to unveiling our hearts. That process is central to an image that St. Paul also used (2 Cor. 3:12-18). He compared the denseness of those who heard the Pentateuch read but closed their hearts and minds to its implications to be "Like Moses, who put a veil over his face so that the Israelites could not look intently." As a result of this veiling, "their thoughts were rendered dull," and "a veil lay over their hearts" (v.14, 15).

People may not know why their understanding of the parables and the biblical stories is veiled. Many psychotherapeutic assessment tools can help identify some of those blockages. So, in addition to the more traditional discernment and formation tools offered by the church, instruments such as the Rorschach, the TAT (Thematic Apperception Test), the Weschler suite of tests, and countless other normed tests can offer precise areas for focusing psychotherapy.

Each parable calls any who hear it to ever more profound commitment. If anyone refuses to be open-hearted, Jesus' paradoxical stories come across to them as God's judgment. Jesus' stories starkly signal the need for repentance from all stubbornness and sin.

The purpose of discernment is to learn what God wants of us and for us. That is because holiness lies in doing God's will (DeCaussade, 2013). Hankle (2013, p. 17) added more specifically that according to Ignatius of Loyola, the purpose of discernment is to know with certitude if a person is acting on one's own spirit, the spirit of God, or the spirit of darkness. As mentioned, for those trained in their use, many psychological assessment tools can unveil a client's motivation and reveal psychological issues that mask spiritual issues.

For those open to Jesus' parables, the Holy Spirit removes the veil over our minds and hearts. Indeed, whenever a person turns to the Lord, Jesus' words and stories remove those veils over our minds and hearts. Through the power of His stories, the Spirit grants access to the knowledge of His kingdom. Thus, our task is to beg the Spirit of the Lord to increase our freedom so that "All of us, gazing with unveiled face on the glory of the Lord" experience transformation into the image and glory of "the Lord who is the Spirit" (v. 18).

Our stories and the effect of media today veiling our consciousness is the theme of *Veils of Distortion* (Zada, 2021). Through fake news and even legitimate news, such media foster emotional churning, exaggeration, and a culture of argumentation. Linking "objective news" to endless advertising for products misdirects our vigilance, feeds on fear and anxiety, and shapes news to reinforce the expectations of the channel's demographic. All these influences are constant and primarily unconscious.

Without the help of the Holy Spirit, the daily distortions all around us veil the intent of Jesus' stories. Parables use simple-sounding stories that involve Jesus' hidden wisdom, and they enable us to live the Great Commandment on Jesus' terms if understood.

Because the parables are kingdom stories, to understand them more profoundly, we must beg the Holy Spirit to show them to us.

Have you had a time in your life where your understanding was veiled or where your response to God's will was ambivalent? How did your lack of insight or ambivalence influence the course of your life? When? Where? How? What was your need? Your apostolate?

Continue to work on your story. People need to hear our stories, your stories. I've told mine and can share more, but will you share your story?

Stories (Biesenbach, 2018):

➢ Cause our brains to produce oxytocin, a chemical related to empathy and a desire to cooperate (p. 12)

➢ Get to the heart of it (p. 14)

➢ Put a face on it, connect us, humanize us, accomplish "show, don't tell" (p. 15-6).

➢ For more tips, please see the *Telling Our Stories* worksheet #2.

Why "our stories?"

As Aslan, the lion, the Christ figure in C.S. Lewis', *The Horse and His Boy (Chronicles of Narnia, #5)*, the hero had asked about someone they met on their adventure, "Child," said the Lion, "I am telling you your story, not hers. No one is told any story but their own."

Sharing and hearing stories are one "language" through which clients and psychotherapists can speak to one another. So, I invite you to "hear" and, if you choose, to tell your story of your adventure with God. No one can "hear" or tell your story but you. If the Spirit helps you to hear your story and tell it is to find God's action, wisdom, and power for holiness in the events of your life.

God knows and loves your story. Do you?

Do you want to understand people today? Then, empathize with their stories. To do that, let the Spirit teach you to speak of your story.

Begin with whatever incident in your life may have come to mind in this chapter.

    a. What was good about it?

    b. What was bad about it?

    c. How was God present for you in it?

Figure 8: Skeptics confusion. 123rf.com

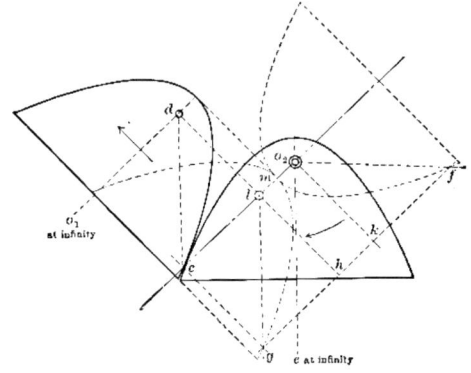

Figure 8

Skeptics confusion.

123rf.com

8

THE SKEPTICS VERSUS THE CHILDLIKE

Resistance, skepticism, and confusion are weeds that readily creep into our thinking if discernment is thought of as a one-and-done event rather than a complex and life-long process. Psychological and spiritual disciplines create a spirit turned to God (Hankle, 2013, p. 23) that requires lifelong learning (Roberto, 2022).

The Bible marked resistance and skepticism as signifying a spiritually veiled or hardened heart. ACT refers to resistance and skepticism psychologically as experiential avoidance.

ACT psychotherapists (Hayes, Strosahl, & Wilson, 2012, pp. 12, 24, ff.) deal with avoidance by moving step-by-step toward a more desirable life outcome. From the ACT perspective, experiential avoidance is a process in which "unpleasant events are ignored, distorted, or forgotten" (p. 73). Though such avoidance can be adaptive when people first struggle to integrate traumatic events a bit at a time rather than becoming overwhelmed, it prevents healing in the long run. Yet, in the end, resistance to therapy is understandable in the context of experiential avoidance.

ACT stresses the need for therapist compassion and acceptance of where the client is as essential for reducing the stigma of psychological problems and then facilitating the sorting out of thinking, feeling, and acting (p. 90).

The adaptation process involves the client gradually embracing the unwanted and distressing event in stages (p. 114-116). To successfully adapt to harmful circumstances, a client must recognize the cost of previous self-help strategies and then move toward a successful strategy even if that entails abandoning previous rule systems (p. 167-168).

Clients need help staying in the present moment during the psychotherapy process. So, good therapists gently bring them back to the "here and now" from the "there and then." Waiting for clients to move on their own toward attentional control will likely prove disappointing for the therapist (p. 206).

The biblical story that illustrates the effect of cynicism on our judgment is visible in Jesus' response to the scorn of **the children in the marketplace** (Luke 7:31-35). Jesus taught (Blomberg, 2012, pp. 266, ff.) that (1) The joyful message of forgiveness should be freely celebrated and not dampened by legalistic restrictions. (2) The solemn message of repentance should not be ignored but taken with full seriousness. (3) The truth of both principles will be demonstrated by those who implement them. Skeptics avoid all three of these. They joylessly make forgiveness more complicated; they discount any urging toward repentance and ignore the words and examples of those who seek God's forgiveness. Most importantly, they ignore their own need for repentance. They are blinded because they negate Zacharias' promise that God will "give his people knowledge of salvation by the forgiveness of their sins" (Luke 1:77).

To the skeptics, all is a joke, an obstacle, while Jesus consistently urges us to let go of negative thoughts to follow him (Luke 18:24-34). In comparing the skeptics to the childlike, Jesus repeatedly pointed to children and held up their spontaneous responses to his followers as examples.

Jesus repeatedly used what Jeremias (1963, pp. 227-229) calls parabolic actions, behaviors that are visible demonstrations of Kingdom values. For example, he pointed to children's openness and vulnerability in response to skeptical questions. In this case, it was an argument among the disciples about who was the greatest. In highlighting the candidness of children, Jesus aligned himself with those who allow themselves to be amazed by God's actions.

A similar skepticism accounts for spiritual blindness. Jesus repeatedly cited his use of stories to help us discern the difference between the skeptical and the childlike. He warned the skeptics that their cynicism would render them unable to internalize or understand his message (Luke 8:9).

When the skeptical serve rather than criticize, their status before God changes from least in status to the greatest status in Jesus' kingdom (Luke 9:46-47). In psychotherapy, clients likewise find healing and integration to the degree that they turn away from avoidance and resistance (Amador, 2012).

A comparison of the skeptical versus the childlike looks like this.

The childlike vs. the skeptical	
The Childlike	**Skeptics**
Agree to be led	Resist being led
Are like a healthy tree	Are like a rotten tree
Are like sheep	Are like wolves
Bear fruit for God	Bear weeds and thistles
Are true and humble	Are standoffish and superior
Serve rather than criticize	Criticize but do not serve
Are hidden in God	Are visible to the world
Trust that God save will	Will discover that God will cut down
Will enter the Kingdom of God	Will not enter the kingdom of God
Are the Greatest before God (Luke 9:46-47)	Are the least before God

Discernment is necessary for psychotherapists because clients frequently present with frantic attempts to avoid pain, slowing down the process can be helpful and necessary for healing in the person's life (Hayes, Strosahl, & Wilson, 2012, p. 210).

When clients slip out of the present moment or seem to "zone out," a therapist can gently call the client back by asking, "What just came up for you just now?" (p.267).

Skeptics are typically too much with us. Their negative and skeptical comments frequently fill the news.

Here, our contrast model can be Job. Though the initial scene in heaven showed that Job was innocent, the prodding of the heavenly council demanded that God defend his policies on permitting suffering. The four friends are examples of all the attitudes of resistance, avoidance, and skepticism in Job's time and ours. Even the appearance of God at the end of the book of Job offers little comfort. God answered that God is God, and we are not. God asked whether Job was present when God planned and created the universe. Of course, he was not, and neither were we.

Today's avoiders, questioners, and doubters might have different understandings of suffering. However, like Job, it can be a struggle to modify their negative, avoidant, and cynical thinking. Instead, ACT proposes that we move toward our problems rather than avoid them. Approaching can help with mental health and help us experience God's saving help at each step into the future.

We tell our stories in the face of skepticism and cynicism of the world. However, to be fair to the world, thinking we can find wisdom and discernment on our own violates a principle St. John, the Evangelist (1 John 4:1) taught. Namely, if someone acknowledges Jesus as coming in the flesh, that is, God present among us, they are on the right path. If they do not recognize him, they are off the path to life and lose the ongoing help available to those who consciously intend to remain "in Christ." As soon as we are not following Jesus' word, for example, we are beginning to drift away from God's hope and plan for us. He warned us to "test the spirits" of the world to see whether they belong to God.

Now consider your story. (Biesenbach, 2018). Perhaps one or another of these questions will help you get started on your story.

Have you allowed Jesus' words or Mary's example to guide you?

Have you been more like the skeptics or more like the childlike?

Have you experienced inner conflicts between your inner skeptic and your daughter or son of God?

When you set high-stakes goals, did you allow God to have a hand in those goals, or did you try to do everything yourself?

Have you noticed cause and effect challenges and results when allowing God to have a place in your life and even in your practice versus when you allowed God no place in those life experiences?

Can you identify emotionally charged decisions and resolutions where you allowed God a role compared to when you decided alone without God?

Luke (18:15-17) repeated Jesus' action of pointing to a child, not just as an ideal but also as a necessity. He stressed that whoever did not accept his words and intentional actions like a child would not enter his new kingdom.

Remember that stories locate us and integrate us with our environments. You show how you connect to your unique environment and, thus, a model for others by telling your narrative.

Was there a moment in which your inner child and inner skeptics battled for dominance?

    a. What was good about it?

    b. What was bad about it?

    c. How was God present for you in it?

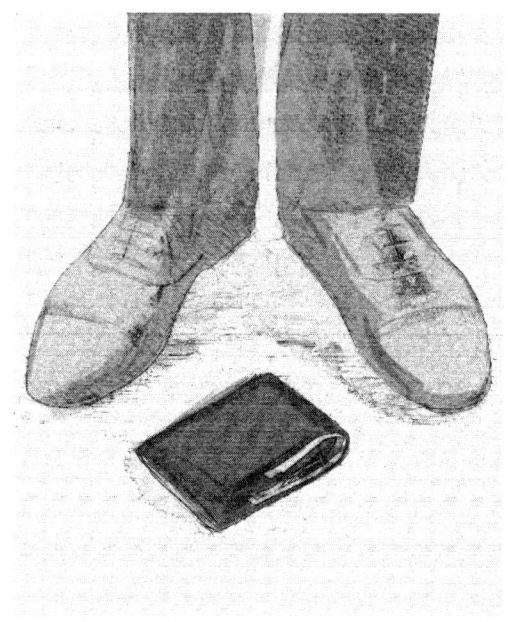

Figure 9

Lost values.

James Jasper

9

STORYTELLING AND THE RCIA

When we consider lost values and lost people, we might debate whether people get lost in life and then lose their values or lose their values and then get lost in life. Either way, the two parables in this chapter, **the lost sheep, and the lost coin** (Luke 15:1-10), are like bookends and can be read with either considered first or the other following. The number of people in either category is countless. I propose that we focus on those who have drifted away from God spiritually and religiously and present for mental health psychotherapy.

Linking the parable of **the ten coins** (Luke 19:11-27) with the two "lost" stories can seem like an improbable joining. However, this central parable stresses that our obligation to God is a major theme in Jesus' parables. The image of loaned money clarifies that there is no excuse for not using the valuable coins and talents God has given us.

Remember, in these parables, there is no definition of means, time frames, quality, or proportionality to the coin-gifts. That is, God gives us skills and abilities and then keeps score on our use of them.

For demonstration purposes, I will ask you to consider that one use of the gifts entrusted to us might include helping any parish with the inquiry and mystagogy periods of the RCIA (National Conference of Catholic Bishops, 1988).

Two of Jesus' parables, the **lost sheep and lost coin parables** (Luke 15:1-10), speak not only of sheep wandering off but can analogously refer to all the people searching for a sense of purpose and direction in life.

In this analogy, Jesus' demonstrated his astonishing concern and willingness to search out those who have lost their way.

Blomberg (2012, p. 214) pointed out that just as the shepherd went out of his way to search diligently for his lost sheep, God takes the initiative to go to great lengths to seek and save the lost who have wandered away from God or lost interest in living. Whatever the circumstances or priority, God does not abandon them, and neither can we. Jesus calls us to compassion for those struggling with mental health issues such as anxiety, depression, serious and chronic mental illness, chemical dependency, personality disorders, and family, marital, and social conflicts.

Further, just as the discovery of the lost sheep elicited great joy, the salvation of lost men and women is a cause of celebration. We do well to rejoice when those who have been wandering find health, a sense of direction, or a sense of self as valuable.

The safety of the many is no excuse for not searching for those who are lost, those who claim to be God's people must not impede the helping professions to rescue more. Therapists who work for psychological and spiritual health and peace may be the only ones with whom clients will have meaningful contact.

Snodgrass (2018, pp. 519-543) wrote that there is no excuse for not using our "coins," that is, talents, regardless of how many "coins" God has given us. The principle Jesus proclaimed is that "to everyone who has, more will be given, but from the one who has not, even what he has will be taken away" (v. 26).

The coins parable also points to stewardship now and evaluation of success later. In Luke, the master, Jesus, is present now and in the future as judge and accountant of God's loans. The master spared the third servant who had only minimal talent but judged and severely punished rebellious servants.

Snodgrass (p. 542) added that knowledge of God's reign and salvation brings with it added responsibility. To accept the kingdom and its salvation is to assume responsibility. We either become agents of the kingdom, and God rewards us, or we refuse, and God will judge us in terms of our faithfulness to life tasks. Regardless of how many coins we have received, we are all responsible for doing our small part in God's vast intergalactic plan. Our goal is that God finds us blameless because of our justice, mercy, truth, and gentleness in life.

To avoid or resist Jesus' terms for using our coins (abilities) to search for lost sheep (people) and coins (values) is to resist the will of the Father. We cannot and should not judge others, but we can compassionately warn them that according to Jesus, their situation is dangerous.

To connect these parables with discernment we can add that ACT psychological principles offer concrete strategies for the task of acceptance versus experiential avoidance. Acceptance here means "willingness to make contact with inner experiences without efforts to escape, change, or control events" (Stoddard & Afari, 2014, pp. 7-12). Accepting is the opposite of walking away.

Hayes, Strosahl, and Wilson's (2012) principles apply psychotherapeutic strategies to Jesus' three parables–the coins, lost sheep, and ten coins--that effective ACT psychotherapy must include the following.

- ✓ ACT therapists develop a relationship with clients that come out of the CBT traditions of theory, practice, and hopeful outcomes.

- ✓ ACT therapists share in the suite of techniques that fill countless therapists' books and training.

- ✓ ACT therapists integrate identity, interpersonal skills, Christian and psychotherapeutic values, and strategies for coping with our current environments.

- ✓ ACT therapists view psychotherapeutic techniques and experience interactions with clients as an art form with the Wisdom tradition in mind.

- ✓ Further, from ancient times Catholic theologians have considered discernment in applying faith and therapy as a gift from the Spirit rather than something we acquire totally through effort and practice (Hankle, 2013, p. 17).

The Association for Catechetical Ministry (ACM, undated online article) is concerned that an unacceptable number of new Catholics stop practicing the Faith soon after reception into the Church through the RCIA process. The association member reported that the neophytes did not reach the necessary informed consent, a problem Sts. John Newman and John Paul II identified (Biersbach, 2021). Without that integration, ACM asserts that the newly baptized become liturgical people and fail to integrate all the moving pieces in the mystery of the faith in their first year after baptism.

For those unfamiliar with the RCIA process, there are four periods: 1) inquiry, 2) catechumenate, 3) enlightenment, and 4) mystagogy. To the credit of those who labor in the RCIA process, ACM has observed that the second and third periods are frequently more developed than the first and fourth. ACM asserts that more profound exploration is necessary for the inquiry period and more thorough mentoring and integration in the mystagogy stage.

For example, when a person calls to enter the church and a parish staff member says they will get back to them in September when the RCIA starts. That is an example of using a school-year model for the RCIA. Another example is that far too frequently no ongoing program to mentor the newly baptized exists after the Easter vigil celebration. Further, the lack of storytelling instills an insufficient sense in the newly baptized that the task of becoming an informed and motivated Catholic requires a commitment to lifetime learning (Roberto, 2022).

It is like saying to a person with a new medical degree that they have finished their courses and should go practice somewhere without the benefit of an internship, residency, or fellowship.

Psychotherapists learn to apply their academic learning during internships and licensing preparation. CPA members might be of help in mentoring new Catholic Christians.

A four-step storytelling process applied to the RCIA would involve

1. concrete exploration in the inquiry (a.k.a., precatechu-
    menate) period,

2. structuring in the catechumenate period,

3. symbolizing during the enlightenment period and

4. mentoring/integration in the mystagogy period.

The focus in the inquiry stage should aim to develop an inquiring perspective that repeatedly asks about incidents past, present, and future, what was good, what was bad about it, and where God was and is in the person's life. Duggan's (1997) book on the precatechumenate is still valuable and Roberto (2022) has admirably expanded on the earlier work of others by citing theory, resources, and teachable moments for lifelong learning and growth in faith.

The focus in the mystagogy stage is to help people experience growth in the Christian life and find resources through the help of the Holy Spirit (Photios, 2005) and the Eucharist (Ostdiek, 2015). Without post-baptismal guides to show them (Romans 10:14), the skeptics, cynics, and misleading media examples steal away what they have heard.

Developing the RCIA inquiry and mystagogy periods and lifelong learning initiative and linking those programs to initial and advanced storytelling is challenging. CPA members may well be limited in the content of such efforts. However, the skill set to listen for subtle cues and attend to God's presence during every life moment requires unique skill-sets that CPA members know well. Further, Catholic psychotherapists sharing those skills in psychotherapy practice and parish work, such as the RCIA can facilitate the lifelong faith growth of others and strengthen their faith growth.

In our stories, we might notice what is perhaps the most common theme in the wisdom literature and the history of the laity in Church history has been the development of a sense of **divine presence**. In the OT (Hamilton, 2008), God was present in the temple, and in the NT, Jesus brought God's presence within us. However, in both the OT wisdom books as well as popular lay piety, metaphors and stories have connected the blessings of divine presence to all aspects of life.

In your experience or your clients' experiences, have there been periods of wandering away from God, self, and others that a sense of God's presence remedied? When, where, and how did that wandering happen in your story or the stories of others? Has a sense of God's presence helped you during painful experiences?

As you sort through incidents in your life and work at telling your stories, cut the exposition (Biesenbach, 2018)**, "I want to tell you." Instead, jump in with one brief sentence.**

- ° **Begin work on your story with a short outline of your anecdote.**
- ° **Then focus on one character.**
- ° **Avoid tangents: go in a straight line.**
- ° **Stick to clear turning points.**

Summarize by asking if there were moments in your event that illustrated how a sense of God's presence provided what you needed in that time?

a. What was good about it?

b. What was bad about it?

c. How was God present for you in it?

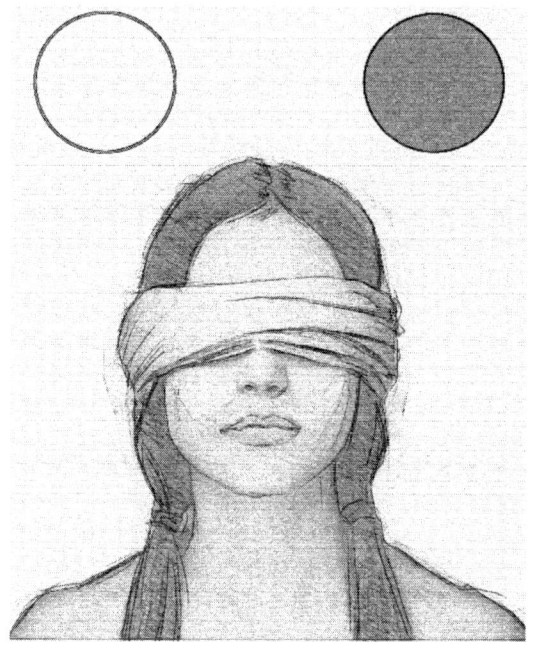

Figure 10

Choosing the good.

James Jasper

10

SALT AND
REDISCOVERING VIRTUE

After Virtue, the title of MacIntyre's book, says it all (1981, 1984, 2007). In it, he traced the consequences of relativism and scientism in western societies that led to the passing away of a shared sense of value and virtue to a more current loss of an object or goal for good behavior.

The shift away from valuing virtue recalls Jesus' parables of **the lost coin and lost sheep** (Luke 15:1-10). For some, society's search for values is like the strenuous efforts of the woman who lost a coin. Like the searching woman, theorists sweep their houses and light the lamps with their insights, searching for a lost valuable. In this case, the lost value is knowing the goal of virtuous behavior.

MacIntyre's analysis of philosophical and ethical trends documented that the sense of virtuous practice and the traditional interpretation of virtue in multiple circumstances has evaporated (MacIntyre, 1981, 1984, 2007).

In his telling, new philosophies since the European enlightenment of the 18th century offered rival and contradictory understandings of virtue (p. x). To repair and propose new understandings of virtue, philosophers more recently have looked to Aristotle, Buddhism, American utilitarianism, or liberalism (p. xiii-xv). However, none have proved sufficient to sustain families, local communities, and national societies. Macintyre expressed hope to return to monastic life by reflecting on prayer, learning, and labor (p. xvi). However, his "solution" sounds like the 1961 musical, *Stop the World I Want to Get Off*. Rather, Macintyre's own words regarding the current state of virtue sound on the mark, "we are all already in a state so disastrous that there are no large remedies for it" (p. 5).

Jesus' simile of salt "Salt is good, but if salt itself loses its taste, with what can it's flavor be restored?" (Luke 14:34-35) is a one-sentence declaration that "if Jesus' disciples fail to live up to their calling, there is no one else for the world to count on for similar tasks" (Blomberg, 2012, p. 402).

Pope Benedict XVI's book on Christians as the salt of the earth (Ratzinger, 1997) listed a range of problems in our time that illustrate the necessity of Christians to have a taste for virtue in a secular world that is like adding salt for flavor.

Seewald had asked (p. 261), "Is a new tone, a new sound, needed in the handing on of the faith?" Ratzinger answered with a very concrete example. He said,

Yes, I think so. I read the story of an orthodox priest who said: 'I have tried so hard, but the people simply don't listen to me; they simply don't listen to me; they go to sleep, or simply don't come at all.'

Ratzinger added, "That is an example of experiences that others have too."

Pope Benedict reflected that because of relativism and rampant scientism everyone has their truth and worldview. He reserved special blame for rampant scientism that only acknowledges the observable and measurable as genuine and relevant. He asserted that, like salt adding zest and favor, the antidote to relativism and scientism is to develop habits of doing what is right, and those habits the Church refers to as virtue.

Jesus' salt parable prompts us to ask how relativism and scientism become such powerful influences?

I found an answer rooted in a mixture of history and philosophy in Gregory's book (2012), *The Unintended Reformation*. The book cleverly linked moments in history and philosophy over the last 500 years that altered social consciousness in six steps.

First, Luther was surprised that others went in every direction within 10-20 years of posting his theses (Gregory, 2012, pp. 89, 91, 205)

Second, the religious wars, such as the 30-years war (1618-1648), persisted until Europe was exhausted from the terrible devastation as Catholics and Protestants bloodied one another until whole regions were nearly depopulated (Gregory, 2012, pp. 112-113, 159-160, 273-274).

Third, to stop the conflicts and control the religiously motivated uprisings of churches, a consensus grew that believers should practice religion only in private to avoid bloody open war. The Medieval view had fused faith and politics. However, after the 30-years war and to achieve civil order, public sentiment banished faith from the public square. Instead, personal piety displaced public expressions of devotion to dampen religious zealotry. Thus, civil gatherings of public will as expressions of democratic vote replaced religious rituals (Gregory, 2012, pp. 129-179). A widespread longing to re-insert religion into politics persists even today for fervent believers who hope for an American theocracy expressing whatever their brand of faith might be (Phillips K. , 2006).

Fourth, philosophers arose who discounted faith. To fill the faith gap, philosophers had as a starting point the conviction that each author needed to devise a new philosophy of life from scratch. Each philosophical system argued convincingly of the validity of their approach. However, none of the philosophies agreed with the other (Gregory, 2012, pp. 181-234). Instead, the standards for each perspective became dependent on subjective criteria, "What I think is…" or "What I argue for is…."

Fifth, reacting to no general agreement on morality, society's focus shifted to material well-being. In the Unintended Reformation, Gregory called the trend "manufacturing the Goods Life" (2012, pp. 235-297). Instead of virtue, material well-being became the substitute.

Sixth, the last step was to abandon wisdom in favor of knowledge (Gregory, 2012, pp. 298-364). For example, just after 1825, the universities of London, Cambridge, and Oxford refused Darwin's world-changing 25,000 biological samples judging Darwin's studies "not fit study for a gentleman." However, by 1850 all three universities offered terminal applied degrees in the sciences.

Since then, many universities continue to shift from pursuing wisdom in favor of responding to social norms and career development. Increasingly those social norms are "an ethical theory that regards ethical and value judgments as expressions of feeling or attitude and prescriptions of action, rather than assertions or reports of anything" (Online dictionary). Everything is either opinion or empirically validated research results. The largest universities now seek new knowledge within departments siloed into lessened contact with other disciplines.

Gregory (2012, pp. 364-387) accurately asserted that what is left is a nostalgic longing for the moral certainty of the past and a rejection of the 500 years that got us here. I propose that acknowledging the reality of the history that got us here is a step toward an antidote. Jesus' counter-culture parables and biblical stories are all concrete, interpersonal, and cast in social situations with context as the scientists seek, but full of certitude instead of relativism.

The ACT psychotherapeutic approach likewise works toward acceptance versus avoidance, present moment awareness versus attachment to conceptualized past and feared future, clarity of values versus relativism, and flexibility in application that considers the context of individuals.

I find the hope of a return to Aristotle's terms and world-view on virtue improbable. Try reading Macintyre's analysis of Aristotle and see if you come to the same conclusion that learning his definition of terms is a confusing quagmire and speaks of social understandings of ages long past.

For example, Aristotle's definition of friendship is radically different from current understandings of it. Or, again, faith, hope, and charity are central to our understanding of virtue, but Aristotle scarcely mentions them (p. 182-183). Even Jane Austin's attempt at virtue definitions such as "constancy," is a concept since lost to our mobile society. The current media neither emphasizes nor mentions teleology, the purpose of reality, and the supernatural to support modern virtue.

Also, Aristotle's list of virtues is not the only one. As MacIntyre observed in After Virtue, thinkers as diverse as Homer, Socrates, the authors of the New Testament, Thomas Aquinas, and Benjamin Franklin all have their lists.

Further, MacIntyre praised the alternative work of Peterson and Seligman in 2004 listed virtues in a modern, empirical, and rigorously scientific manner that is also in line with most cultures throughout history. Plus, their six classes of core virtues and twenty-eight measurable "character strengths" intend to increase experiences of happiness consistent with both the authors' theoretical framework and application to positive psychology.

The problem is that since the Enlightenment, the powerful influence of tradition as a shared sense of values in society has shifted from social values to individual or personal values. Even speaking of the common good is taboo to modern western politics in the age of the individual.

To further underscore the shift to individual focus for virtue is the emergence since 2006 of a blockchain process (McFarland, 2021). Blockchain means that when individuals search the internet, what each person finds is tailored and individualized for that person. Algorithms mediate search results to confirm each person's biases and distortions to their search. The result is that internet searches that many hoped would widen people's perspectives instead bind searchers to their prejudices. Governments are gradually trying to figure out how to modulate the divisive effects of social media platforms.

Social media using blockchain isolates and blinds each person further by linking the searcher to other like-minded individuals. As McFarland (2021) wrote, blockchain is a battle for viewers and minds where each person lives in a world all their own, tailored to their preferences (NYT today, article) so that no two people share the same information or worldview. The result is that everyone's isolation is profound.

In telling our stories we do well to remember that the word "virtus" in Latin means strength. What has been your experience with your moral and psychological strength as being Christian "salt" that adds the zest of virtue to the world? How have you tried to "hear" the signs of the times? Do you find the environment around you to be a world "After Virtue," as MacIntyre suggests?

So, where to begin? Salzman and Lawler (2018, pp. 72-75) pointed to

"Alasdair Macintyre's *After Virtue* (that) identified three logical steps in virtue— 1) practice, 2) narrative order of a single human life, and 3) moral tradition." What has been your experience with?

1. Practicing virtue?
2. Identifying your morality and virtue principles?
3. What guide do you draw from to direct your morality and virtue?

In telling our stories, focus on details that separate the good from the bad.

- **Use 1-3 brief details to set the scene.**

- **Offer sensory details—an image, a memory, a taste, a smell, something touched—to bring a story to life.**

Was there a moment in that event for you that illustrates your need for clear virtuous goals in a values-diluted world?

a. What was good about it?

b. What was bad about it?

c. How was God present for you in it

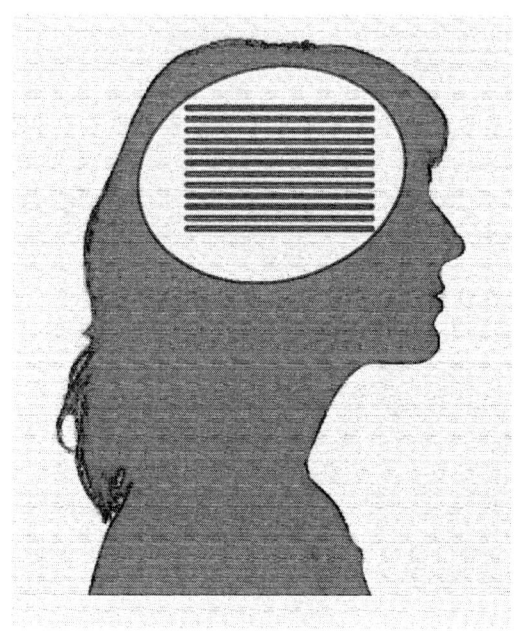

Figure 11

Discerning Virtue.

James Jasper

11

FORGIVENESS AS FIRST STEP TO THE VIRTUES

Many people search for forgiveness, but many other people never forgive. Rather, they live lives filled with resentments, anger, grievance, and victimhood. We are all somewhat broken, but even broken, God wants us. A wonder to me is that God finds ways to work with my brokenness and provide me with constant help, healing, and productivity.

MacNutt (1974, 1999, p. 129) said in his incomparable treatise on healing that the problem with forgiveness, as in all healing, is that, "...one of the real problems we see in the ministry of healing is a problem we find in every area of human activity: a tendency to oversimplify." People are complex, not simple. As Jeremiah (17:9) said, "More tortuous than anything is the human heart, beyond remedy; who can understand it?"

The Catechism (United States Catholic Conference, 1995, pp. 396-415) lays out the Catholic understanding of sacramental penance for the penitent, the confessor, and in terms of the role of the Holy Spirit in effecting forgiveness. That is terrific. However, not everyone gets to sacramental penance. They may be from any number of other religious traditions, have no religious tradition, come from a Christian but not Catholic background, or if Catholic may not be practicing. Most people who need or even seek the healing of forgiveness may quite likely never find their way to sacramental penance.

We do well here to remember that in the Apostles Creed forgiveness of sin is an article of faith. Not everyone accepts that article of faith.

For practicing Catholics, individual and sacramental penance is straightforward, but for everyone else, repentance is more complicated and varies for individuals and social groups. For example, reconciliation can be a complex puzzle for unmarried couples or irregular marriages, even for diocesan tribunals. Finding forgiveness and reconciliation for clans, neighborhoods, regional states, and nations is exponentially more complex, even as it is essential to prevent war, hunger, environmental degradation, or economic disasters.

It is this social healing and need for forgiving and forgiveness that the popes routinely address. In one of his latest works, Pope Francis (2020) proposed a three-step process for healing/forgiveness, namely, see, choose, and act. So, the first step is to see or "unveil" our veiled consciousness. The second, to choose is integral to every parable of Jesus and the ACT process. Each of Jesus' parables presses us to choose God's will over our own. The psychological ACT processes likewise underscore the reality that many clients are aware of their symptoms but either neglect to mindfully reflect on what the symptoms mean or refuse to undertake the actions that could reduce those symptoms.

The result is that many people live consumed by resentment, complaints of deprivation, anger, grievance, and victimhood. Psychotherapy aims to treasure clients who present with a desire to search for forgiveness or purpose of amendment in psychotherapy, whether presenting with anxiety, depression, trauma, addiction, couple therapy, or family therapy. All these conditions can be helped with forgiveness and are further complicated by the lack of reconciliation.

Jesus' parable of the two debtors (Matthew 18:23-35) "(1) The first section magnificently illustrates the boundless grace of God in forgiving sins, as the king forgave his servant. (2) In the middle section, the second servant underlies the absurdity of grace spurned; one who has been forgiven so much and yet so mistreats his fellow debtor does not deserve to live. (3) The final section depicts the frightful fate awaiting the unforgiving, as the wicked servant discovered to his ruin" (Blomberg, 2012, p. 319).

For the unforgiving servant, imprisonment, even if not physical, certainly exists within each person's conscience. However, since the unforgiving does not "see" their blindness the parable pictures them tortured by the master. At death God's grace will no longer be available but, in the meantime, "The kingdom comes with limitless grace amid an evil world, but with it comes limitless demand" (Snodgrass, 2018, p. 72). Because of Jesus' words, churches and individuals should be a continual supply of mercy and forgiveness, mirroring God's character and treatment of his people' (p. 76).

Blomberg (2012, p. 224) says of the two debtors (Matthew 18:23-35) that "This is a juridical parable," that is, "(1) Like the man owing fifty denarii, those who take their spiritual condition for granted and are not aware of being forgiven for numerous gross wickednesses should not despise those who have been redeemed from a more pathetic state. (2) Like the debtor owing five hundred denarii, those who recognize they have much for which to be thankful will naturally respond in generous expressions of love for Jesus. (3) Like the creditor, God forgives both categories of sinners and allows them to begin again with a clean slate."

In asking Simon, the host of the banquet, which would love more, Jesus was clear that the more we are forgiven, and experience our forgiveness, the more we love and can love others.

As Blomberg emphasized, "Grace and responsibility are not about cheap grace, nor is grace ever without responsibility. Forgiveness is without limits but not without responsibility, confession, truth, and even restitution. These two parables are only two pictures of the many sided-subject of forgiveness" (p. 91). They emphasize that forgiveness is too big and encompassing to be dealt with in one chapter or one book. However, forgiveness for us and forgiveness extended to others is the entry door to virtue just as resentment and unforgiving is the blockage to virtue.

But in forgiveness God "give(s) his people knowledge of salvation by the forgiveness of their sins" (Lk. 1:77).

Jesus underscored that point in saying that we should concentrate on getting the **plank out of our eyes** (Luke 6:42), to unveil our consciousness, before we try to pick the splinter, the imperfections of others, out of others' eyes.

Instead, we tend to want to figure out "who's to blame." I must confess that for many years after a long day of doing psychotherapy I would get home late, all wound up, tired, but not ready for bed. So, for an hour or so I would read a murder mystery of some sort. It was reassuring that once the body was found the story would irreversibly press on until the detective or some other hero figured out "who done it." That was most unlike psychotherapy with living clients for whom there were always lots of "loose ends."

To put forgiveness and virtue into perspective it can help to hear what Jesus stressed, namely what comes out of us, namely, evil thoughts, unchastity, theft, murder, adultery, greed, malice, deceit, licentiousness, envy, blasphemy, arrogance, and folly (Mark 7:20-23).

Our focus should be on what behaviors, motives, and reactions come out of us rather than fetishizing other people's behaviors, motives, and reactions.

Discernment around the forgiveness parables, as (Hankle, 2013, p. 21) reminds us, includes not becoming over- or under-focused on the cognitive or thinking aspects of reconciliation.

Underemphasizing the knowledge and thinking aspects of sin and forgiveness can mean that the ACT strategies of stepping back and observing our thinking, feeling, and acting rather than reacting impulsively can lead to a "you" that is unable to observe and experience your inner and outer world so that you become aware of self as more than your thinking, feeling, and acting

Overemphasizing those same thinking or cognitive processes can confuse everyone and bury the self in scrupulosity and doubts (Ciarrocchi, 1995) so that the ACT exercises mindfulness with the present focused awareness of degrees of acceptance, defusion, and self-as-context become a necessity.

It can help to reassure both clients and therapists that God wants us to do what we can in this life and leave the rest to the kingdom. As Pope/Saint John Paul put it none of us comes instantly to wholeness. He called that process of moving toward holiness "gradualness" (Echeverria, 2016). Pope Francis picked up on that same theme, the "law of gradualness," in his letter, *Familiaris Consortio, The Fellowship of the Family*, namely, that for all of us progress in the moral, Christian life, is a step-by-step process.

That is, life is a dynamic process. Pope Francis was clear that "This is not a 'gradualness of law' but rather a gradualness in the prudential exercise of free acts on the part of subjects who are not in a position to understand, appreciate, or fully carry out the objective demands of the law" (2016, p. #295). However, a reality that I can confirm in my experience of psychotherapy, he asserted that (paragraph #303 and 305),

> a person not only may be doing the best that he can, but also that such acts, therefore, are not sinful and hence are right for that person, because the person, in his mitigating circumstances, fulfills the ideal as applied by that individual in those limiting circumstances.

Those behaviors are not "ideal" Christian life. God's ideal for us remains but our efforts, as we all know, are limited to our step-by-step progress toward those ideals.

Psychotherapy agrees that virtue is the result of a process rather than an either-or sense that "Either I have virtue, or I don't." For example, Meninger (1996) proposed that psychological forgiveness happened in five steps: claiming the hurt, guilt, victim, anger, and wholeness. He developed and described each step at length with clarity, context, and examples. Since then, the literature on the psychology of forgiveness has grown steadily.

Another example is Enright's (2014) book. It offers a step-by-step empirically validated process for working through resentment displaced as anger into forgiveness and release. His work is theologically solid in that he proactively stressed that forgiveness is a choice, whether to seek forgiveness for our failings or in forgiving the injuries suffered from others. Further, the book offered tools and a roadmap for working through anger and resentment that only a professional schooled in the CBT (cognitive-behavior therapy) tradition could have produced.

A third example is Terkeurst's (2020) book that developed emotional experiences that have application for others. As she put it, forgiveness is "hard to give" but "amazing to get" (p. 7). The work names many of the issues and emotional roadblocks of the bookend processes of giving and receiving forgiveness.

Finally, the Wisdom tradition bursts with images of life. For wisdom, living well before God is the aim, and life as living is the all-encompassing concept (Podrifka, 2008). This tradition stresses that for humans our highest spiritual principles are intended by God to be lived out in concrete even secular realities.

In our stories, why must we aim both to receive and give forgiveness?

One answer is so that we can refuse to live and be bound by our sins or resentment toward others. As Tibbitts wrote (2007, p. 52) forgiving is a choice as much as Joshua chose God and urged the rest of the Israelites to do the same "If it is displeasing to you to serve the Lord, choose today whom you will serve" the God of Israel or foreign Gods. "As for me and my household, we will serve the Lord" (Joshua 24:15). Tibbits continued (p. 67) that for Christians doing "what doesn't come naturally" or "I can forgive but I can't forget" (Terkeurst, 2020) is not enough. "If then my people, humble themselves and pray, and seek my face and turn from their evil ways, I will hear them from heaven and pardon their sins and heal their land" (2 Chronicles 7:14). Note that humbling ourselves leads to both forgiveness from personal sins and forgiveness of the sins of the whole country or land. Tibbitts urges that we think of God, not our grudges (p. 133), "I think of you upon my bed, I remember you through the watches of the night" (Psalm 63:7). That process ensures our prayer, namely, that Our Father forgives us to the degree we forgive others.

Have you had experiences of seeing or giving forgiveness in your life?

Was anything in this chapter true for you? When? Where? How?

In telling our stories focus on details that separate the good from the bad
   i. **simplify dates and be less precise the farther back you go**
   ii. **omit:**
      1. **proper names**
      2. **precise relationship to characters**
      3. **job titles.**

Was there a moment in that event for you that illustrates how God has worked with your strengths, your weaknesses, and been with you in crucial moments or provided what you needed in that time?

   a. What was good about it?

   b. What was bad about it?

   c. How was God present for you in it?

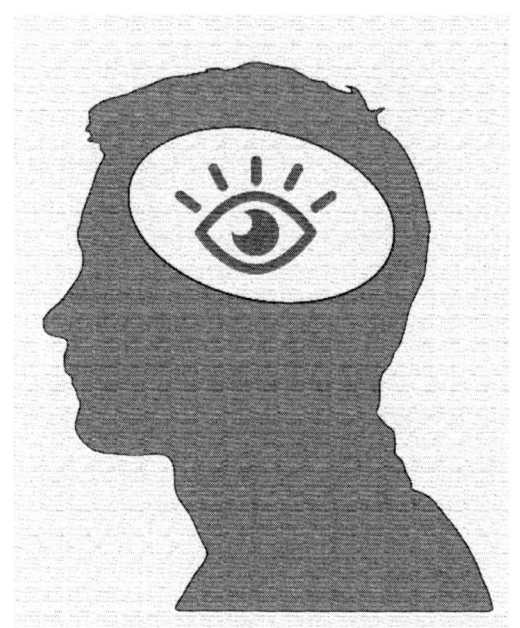

Figure 12

Enlightened by God.

James Jasper

12

THE WORD'S POWER TO ENLIGHTEN

If we seek light in the darkness, we may miss Jesus' **simile of light** (Luke 8:16-18, 11:33-36). The scholars consider it so simple that it scarcely deserves or receives a comment. That is, many commentaries write nothing about the lamp parables, evidently considering them self-evident. However, Pope Benedict XVI wrote a small book on Christians as the light of the world (2010). In it, he reviewed areas needing reform in the church, including what he called "the dictatorship of relativism" (p. 42-59). His diagnosis of what has led to the growth of secularism and relativism is very similar to Gregory's (2012).

Pope Benedict XVI (2010) expanded Luke's themes in the parables and applied them to our current times. He itemized a whole menu of troubles in the world such as climate change (p. 42-49) and what he called "the dictatorship of relativism." The multiple results of relativism have been to darken the world for perceptive souls by insisting that the only light is the light of science. As a further result, Benedict examined what has been the continuing rise of the new atheism (p. 59) and of those who describe their religious practice as "none."

Pope Benedict added that the net result was to cast doubt on truth itself and grant credence to a type of modern secular paganism that has unsettled Catholic Christians. Isaiah (60:2-3, 19c) said, "See, darkness covers the earth, and thick clouds cover the peoples." Yet Isaiah also added a promise,

> But upon you, the Lord shines, and over you appear his glory. Nations shall walk by your light, and kings by your shining radiance. The Lord shall be your light forever, your God shall be your glory.

Our goal here is to ask how we can unveil or enlighten our perspective, our "inner eye."

> Take care, then, how you hear. To anyone who has, more will be given, and from the one who has not, even what he seems to have will be taken away (Luke 8:18).

In support of that, I will hopefully help you hear afresh the parables that you have heard and preached countless times.

> Take care, then, that the light in you not become darkness. If your whole body is full of light, and no part of it is in darkness, then it will be as full of light as a lamp illuminating you with its brightness" (Luke 11:35-36).

In support of that, I will hopefully shine some light on the dark spots in the human condition.

While there are many examples of stories in secular culture and the OT, Jesus' parables, similes, metaphors, and analogies are the most masterful stories. They offer examples of both cognitive and behavioral competencies and can be ideal for interpersonal interaction as well as models of spiritual discernment. Competence is understood as the ability to do something successfully or efficiently. By clinical competence, I mean the ability to practice psychotherapy efficiently and with satisfactory outcomes. Along the way, I will point the reader to a wide array of the best in psychotherapy.

Jesus has two applications for the image of light.

1. One is the **disciple as a lamp** (Luke 8:16-18). If we, as those lamps, are enlightened with Jesus' word, then take care what we hear of his teaching and example because what we have heard will be revealed later and if we have not lit up the world with that revelation, we will lose everything.

2. The other approach (Luke 11:33-36) is to invite us to **light up our inner eye** with the light of Jesus' words

and that light will fill our inner life with brightness. If we do not, our inner life will be in darkness.

Many times, repeated images are paralleled in the OT and would have been common spiritual ideas understood by Jesus' original hearers.

That can be a caution to us. Even if others are leery about the implications of the parables, our thrust must not be to hide what we perceive in peoples' response to the Light that is Jesus' word but to remain a light to the world.

ACT with its starting point of experimental contextualism uses its tools to reduce the distance between "the world and the world as we perceive and interact with it" (Long, 2018, p. 82). The hoped-for result is "contextually based knowledge" (p. 90) that takes on the frequent request to "make it real" whether religiously or psychotherapeutically.

Psychotherapists, therapists, priests, professors, and students, see clients who are blinded, or we might say blindfolded, or at least veiled. They have all sorts of images and sensations (perceptions) shooting around in their heads along with emotional upheaval and perhaps problematic behavior.

Therapists aim to help clients understand themselves just as reading or hearing parables aim to improve our perceptual awareness. The parables are a unique discernment training option for psychotherapists.

> ➤ Parables offer examples of both cognitive and behavioral competencies and can be ideal for interpersonal formation as well as models of spiritual discernment.

> ➤ Parables parallel the profound experiences every psychotherapist has in working with clients.

> ➤ While the parables originated in other cultures and languages, they can translate both language and culture in their applications. They are literary miracles of grace.

➢ By searching for underlying principles in the examination of human behavior, parables parallel case and empirical studies common to psychotherapy research.

➢ Parables share an overabundance of techniques just as ACT techniques, for example, offer plenty of techniques in psychotherapy.

➢ Parable model religious experience embedded in concrete realities and as such stand as remedies for scientism, relativism, secularism, and veiled or blindfolded awareness of the reality of God and the needs of others.

➢ Parables and all the biblical stories share the quality of placing biblical values in a context of discernment that is bigger than ourselves. They help us distinguish between good ideas and God's ideas (Hankle, 2013, p. 17).

➢ In cases where psychotherapists work with the 5-10% of clients who need long-term psychotherapy for more than twenty sessions, the OT wisdom novella provides longer accounts of discernment in difficult times. Hebrews (5:14) called this solid food for the mature, whose faculties have been trained to distinguish good from evil. The novella are short prose fictional narratives intended to edify within an entertaining story (Phillips E. , 2008, p. 495). In short, the novella, like the Bible and the lives of the saints in Church history, provide exactly the kind of context that ACT urges us to attend to.

From a discernment perspective, the intent in parables is like the ACT model that aims to increase flexibility in problem-solving, reduce cognitive fusion (cf. about T-F-A), confront avoidance, and provide a mental health bulwark against the pressures of social expectations.

That is, values too often take a backseat to more immediate goals of being right, looking good, feeling good, defending a conceptualized self, and so on. Beyond relief from psychological pain, people lose contact with what they want in life. Detached from long-term desired qualities of living, patterns of action emerge and gradually dominate in the person's repertoire. Over time, behavioral repertoires narrow and become less sensitive to the current context as it affords valued actions. Persistence and change in the service of effectiveness become less likely. (Hayes S. , Theory of Psychopathology)

Parables momentarily increase curiosity and interest. Growth in interest is an essential step toward that type of motivation that results in commitment and action (Sansone, Geerling, Thoman, & Smith, 2019). In turn, motivation is essential to learning, and learning is essential to acceptance, and commitment to action. As part of that process, interest focuses the person on personal goals, and initial experiences (p. 88-89). However, an individual only finds reasons to persist if the goal has captured their attention (p. 91). Much of that development of interest is unconscious (Anselme & Robinson, 2019, pp. 167-169). However, by introducing interesting stories, Jesus and others who use parables and analogies begin the motivational process if attention and interest are drawn unconsciously to the author's goal.

The ACT model cherishes flexibility. ACT teaches mindfulness skills to help individuals live and behave flexibly in ways consistent with personal values. To develop flexibility, the ACT approach uses a large variety of metaphors (Stoddard & Afari, 2014, pp. 1-4) to use reshaped language to connect clients to the context of their specific situation.

It is noteworthy that religious experience as mediated by language and culture (Biersbach, 2021) is remarkably identical to the ACT emphasis on language and context in psychotherapy.

As an orientation to psychotherapy ACT asserts that psychological suffering comes from people boxing themselves into painful corners. The result is that people

1) avoid what they understand as painful parts of their lives and

2) those painful language traps, inflexible avoidance, attachment to conceptions of the dysfunctional self, loss of contact with the present, and reluctance to take behavioral steps with their true values take over their lives (Hayes S. , The Six Core Processes of ACT).

The Church has much more elegant and complex understandings of human suffering, but ACT is research-based and works in psychotherapy to relieve whole ranges of psychological suffering. Together they form a powerful combination.

An additional advantage of ACT is that a growing body of research supports the assertion that ACT approaches work well with a wide range of people, within multiple cultures, and multiple diagnoses (Hayes, Strosahl, & Wilson, 2012). At present ACT appears to have near-universal applicability.

The intent of our stories, as any great storyteller knows, can get lost if we ramble on or drift into tangents. It is a constant tendency that I must struggle with. When I am writing well, I often cut ten times more than I keep. Instead of wandering, every word, and every sentence must fight for its place on the page. Editing and trimming are painful, hard work but necessary.

In telling your stories, remember to exercise your storyteller editing skills to:

- omit irrelevant details

- compress the timeline

- change the order of events if necessary for clarity's sake.

That's the work of the storyteller who struggles to make their story brief and to the point. The penalty for not doing that is that people tune us out or simply put down what we have written. Even if we do our best, what we write or say may not capture the curiosity or interest of many. Such is the storyteller's challenge.

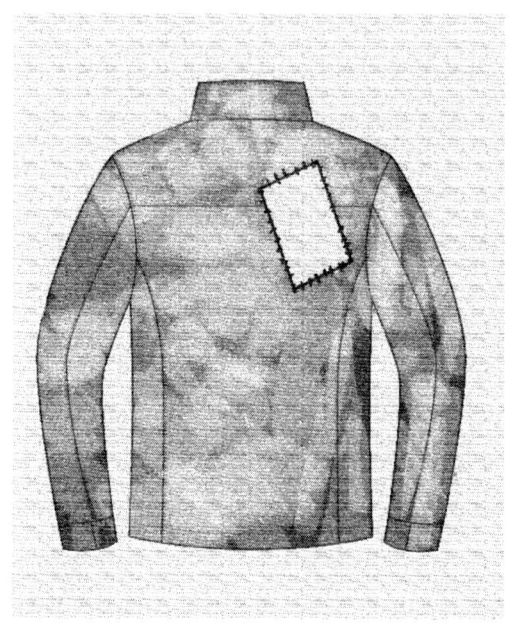

Figure 13

Old and new.

James Jasper

13

ACCEPTANCE OF THE NEW AND THE OLD

The present versus the past is a persistent human preoccupation. The tensions between the here-and-now versus the there-and-then are whether all that is new and shiny is best or that all that is old and traditional is best.

An example of that tension is Pope Francis' (2021) letter on the use of the Roman liturgy as it existed before 1970. His intention was "to promote the concord and unity of the Church, with paternal solicitude towards those who adhere to" the old form. Notice here that the Pope's focus was on unity. Many young people have been clinging to the Latin form for three reasons (Aabram, 2021). First, they found it beautiful, second, it was "rebellion against the modern age," and third, it was "a shortcut to an enthusiastic faith community" with others longing for the older language and religious culture.

The preservation of the Latin form was a temporary accommodation to those "individuals who found serene enjoyment in attending Mass according to the older rites and have no other agenda" (Ferrone, 2021, p. 15). The "no other agenda" was an important caution. The Latin form was preserved to accommodate those who struggled with the new language and reforms. Yet the unintended results were rebellion and the formation of separate communities among rebellious individuals and in three newly formed traditional religious communities (Pentin, 2021). For those groups, the reason for existence was to preserve a language and culture that 99% (Ferrone, 2021) of Catholics had moved on from. Most importantly the traditional movement was frequently and stridently advocating that Vatican II and the current leadership were illicit.

The church tolerated the traditional rite from 1970 to 2021 until that tolerance led to organizational disunion (Ferrone, 2021). The pope acted out of a concern for unity. In effect, he asked the traditionalists to "fast" from their desires for the old to remain part of the living church.

From a social perspective, a strong case can be that an underlying issue for Americans was anxiety over the sense that America was no longer as overtly a Christian country as it once was. Bottum's (2014) book described how mainline Protestant ethic and dominance has fully fizzled away at a time when Catholics were struggling with their issues (Steinfels, 2003). Although Bottum said that "Catholic thought remains the largest and most elaborate intellectual project the world has ever known, dwarfing all the other systems, from Confucianism to Marxism..." (p. 154), he added that the church Paul VI called forth "...that was supposed to go outward instead got turned inward, and what the pope had intended as a confident church acting externally against the injustices of the world became instead an obsessive interiority..." (p. 206). Bottom bemoaned "...the current rage for spirituality without fixed credal content..." (p. 283) and "...the unfettered freedom of the autonomous individual..." (p. 288). In the end, Bottum's book is breathtaking in its vision but is vastly better at identifying the current state of faith struggles and societal drift than in proposing solutions.

However, Bottum's book is clear that this drift in the religious traditions is cause for anxiety and depression for millions of psychotherapy clients. The adaptive psychological response to anxiety and depression is psychological flexibility. The issue at this point is how to connect the psychological aspects of Christian life and prayer to the biological functions of the brain and human behavior (Hankle, 2013, p. 24). Because the ACT model is a help in making those connections that will be a core part of this book.

To be clear, Pope Francis's letter countered the claims of the Latin rite's supporters that Vatican II was valid, that the developments of the Council were appropriate, that the form of worship for the Latin rite was the current Roman Missal, and that it was important for the traditional movement to move on within the life of the living church.

Two parables, **new versus old cloth and new versus old wine** (Luke 5:33-39) speak to an entire range of issues in religious, social, and individual life over time.

The theme played out in Jesus' time. Jesus brought a new realm with a call for sinners to repent–**new wineskins** (Bock, 2012, p. 164). Jesus brought new

perspectives on forgiveness–the new wineskin, new cloth– that cannot mix with the old law/cloth/wineskin (p. 275). Jesus' fresh teachings on the mysterious "kingdom of God" produced reactions from those who liked the old wine–the old law and practices (p. 336).

In time it became clear that those who liked the **old wine** (p. 439) would not try Jesus' new law of love (Luke 5:39). Jesus was clear that the disciple who keeps looking back is not fit for the kingdom (Luke 9:61-62).

In Luke's account the patch piece was torn from the new garment–Jesus' good news–so it is the new garment that suffers to patch the old (Harrington, 1969, p. 1002). People's satisfaction with old forms prevents them from sampling the new and in terms of this example, the new cloth cut out to try to unsuccessfully adapt the old law to the new satisfies neither the old nor the new.

Ivereigh (2018) compared Pope Francis' style to that of a spiritual director accompanying the Church and helping it navigate the trials of a growing, living, organism moving from past to future in healthy development. Along the way, Francis has steered away from the false consolations and temptations of our times but also rejected blind clinging to the past (McEvoy, 2020). Instead, Pope Francis links his position to discernment and conversion.

A dynamic similar to the Church's struggles occurs in political reactions as the traditional and the liberal mindsets have shifted back and forth since the start of the American constitution

(Corey, 2021). However, as many psychotherapists know, individuals, families, and societies can be very resistant to change.

ACT is about the psychological processes that support and enable the possibilities for constructive change, such as, by letting go of the old garment, the old wine, versus clinging to old practices and lifestyles. The ACT theory of psychopathology (Hayes S. , The Six Core Processes of ACT) and ACT protocols target the processes of language that are involved in psychological distress and their remedies. Stated otherwise (Hayes S. , The Six Core Processes of ACT),

> technologically, ACT uses both traditional behavior therapy techniques (defined broadly to include everything from cognitive therapy to behavior analysis), as well as others that are more recent or that have largely emerged from outside the behavior tradition, such as cognitive defusion, acceptance, mindfulness, values, and commitment methods.

In the expanded form the core ACT processes include,

1. Acceptance versus denial: "it takes both wisdom and courage to live a vital life, and our culture offers little guidance on how to do both" (Hayes, Strosahl, & Wilson, 2012, p. 271). We can only begin from where we are. However, to begin we must accept our life as it is. As the therapy adage goes, "Denial is not just a river in Egypt." Half of all those I tried to do ACT with to reduce their symptoms would refuse, even when I would say, "So you would rather have the symptoms than do the work of recovery."

2. Cognitive defusion versus cognitive fusion: "Though suffering is inevitable, there is little point in generating additional suffering through inflexible psychological processes" (Nieuwsma, 2016, p. 209). This ACT process aims to reduce "the domination of stimulus functions based on literal language even when that process is harmful.

3. <u>Psychological flexibility reminds us that we are not the sum of our thinking, feelings, and history</u> (Niemivirta, Pulkka, Tapola, & Tuominen, 2019, p. 212): the domination of a conceptualized self over the "self as context" that emerges from perspective-taking.

4. <u>Fusion vs. defused</u>: Please see worksheet #3, About Thinking, Feeling, and Acting (T-F-A). Sorting through our T-F-A is essential in sorting through all kinds of situations. For example, with those sorting through sexual desires, it can be part of acceptance and commitment to gender to discern "My urges are powerful, and I need to take them into account, but I am not my desires."

5. <u>Being present versus experiential avoidance:</u> present moment awareness is the remedy to the phenomenon that occurs when someone is unwilling to remain in contact with their private experiences and takes steps to alter the form or frequency of these events and the contexts that occasion them, even when doing so causes psychological harm. ADD prayer here.

6. <u>Defining our valued direction versus aimlessness:</u> lack of values, confusion of goals with values, and other values problems can underly the failure to build broad and flexible repertoires.

7. <u>Committed action vs. not taking first steps in a valued direction:</u> inability to build a larger unit of behavior through a commitment to behavior that moves in the direction of chosen values leads to a directionless life.

Any of these ACT processes can contribute to either a psychological or a spiritual discussion of working through distractions and distortions in Christian prayer or the intrusions of expectations past, present, and future into the Christian life.

Our Story's first goal in sorting through the past, present, and future is to understand and discern within our stories. That process can help each of us to first get the plank out of our eye before we try to get the speck out of everyone else's eye.

In telling your story be ruthless in refining and editing (Biesenbach, 2018)**. Nothing kills a story like overstaying your welcome. Brief is best. The hardest task is to be brilliant, be brief, and be seated!**

Was there a moment in that event for you that illustrates how God has worked with your strengths, your weaknesses, and been with you in crucial moments or provided what you needed in that time?

    a. What was good about it?

    b. What was bad about it?

    c. How was God present for you in it?

Figure 14

The Holy Spirit leads to virtue.

James Jasper

14

THE HUMAN CONDITION VS. VIRTUE

Why is change so hard? We humans have spent millennia and formidable effort trying to figure out why life is so hard and why we fail at doing better.

For example, Voltaire (d. 1778) observed that "moral evil is inevitable to human nature" but that even in our weakness humanity is capable of "strength, versatility, and creativity" and because of humanity's possibilities God allows evil (Wiley, 2002, p. 110).

Schelling (d. 1854) added that the mechanism of one action in Genesis understood as visited on succeeding generations has never been clear and without clarity on means of transmission remains "absurd" (Wiley, 2002, p. 111).

Wiley continued that modern science has proposed that the validated research on learning theory and motivation psychology has shifted our reflection on the human condition in new directions. Since God is the source of all truth (Catechism #2465) developmental psychology, learning theory, and motivation must form a renewed foundation when reflecting on the conception of original sin (Wiley, 2002, p. 115). The Catholic church had a bumpy start in dealing with science but more readily accepts that doctrinal pronouncements do not rule out scientific judgments arrived at by methodological observation of empirical data (p. 120), including evolutionary theories (p. 122) and our understanding of human origins. That is, doctrinal discussion of discernment as well as in our understanding of humanity's history must include our biological history (Hankle, 2013, p. 19).

The incorporation of empirical data without rejecting faith and faith without rejecting empirical data remains a pervasive challenge that leaves truth veiled when trying to explain the reality of universal sinfulness.

As Rosemary Ruether observed humanity is "radically alienated" (Wiley, 2002, p. 173) by the rise of "isms" such as racism, nationalism, transgenderism, and too many other "isms" to name. Plus, whole movements have arisen from moral and religious subjectivity that aimed to be holy, loving, and responsible, yet became just the opposite. Those movements were each opposed by rationalists promoting reasonable behavior, and the intellectual elite proposing empirical data (p. 187). For example, as profound a theologian as Lonergan (d. 1984) proposed thinking about original sin as an "incapacity to sustain development" (p. 196).

Over and over the path forward appears clearer, but still so vast in scope as to be complicated and overwhelming. Consider, please, the perspectives of both faith on the one hand and, on the other, the vast psychological research data on humanity's "sustained unauthenticity" (Wiley, 2002, p. 208).

The most influential biblical story of all time is arguably **Adam, Eve, and the image of the tree of life in the garden** (Genesis 2-3). It is dramatic, theatrical dialogue, a graphic story that summarizes so much of human history much longer than back 6,000 years or so.

In the Genesis account, Adam and Eve stood in for our human struggles to avoid turning away from God's law and our mixture of refusal and inability to choose the good (Ellis, 1968). That we struggle so mightily to respond flexibly to the pressures of society and the demands of life should not surprise us.

The church has dealt with those struggles under the heading of original sin. The catechism (United States Catholic Conference, 1995) deals with original sin under the heading of the profound relation of man to God (Catechism #386). The OT tried to understand our human condition in terms of the creation story of Genesis (Catechism #388). Original sin was a long-accepted explanation of humanity's spiritual nature when offered freedom of choice (Catechism #396). The import of the Genesis story and its interpretation throughout Church history was that from the beginning humans preferred themselves to God (Catechism #398).

Part of the Gospel's response to human weakness, unenlightened understanding, and flawed relationships with self and God can be found in the section on the virtues in the Catechism (1995, pp. #1803-1845). The section points us to the goals of the Christian life, (#1803) "Whatever is true, whatever is honorable, whatever is just, whatever is pure, whatever is lovely, whatever is gracious, if there is any excellence, if there is anything worthy of praise, think about these things" (Phil. 4:2).

Rather than proposing individualistic goals that are what each person thinks best, the catechism defines human virtues (#1804) as ideals that are stable "attitudes, …dispositions, habitual perfections of intellect and will that govern our actions, order our passions, and guide our conduct according to reason and faith." The benefits of such strengths/virtues are that "They make possible ease, self-mastery, and joy in leading a morally good life. The virtuous man is he who freely practices the good."

When discerning about our story or others' a factor is the human condition, commonly referred to as original sin.

To be clear, original sin is not something, but the lack of something, namely, an ability to save ourselves or remove all our cognitive distortions, emotional upheavals, and negative behaviors, now or in the future. Nor is original sin a single act at a recent time in human history. Rather, the human condition is complicated by personal sin, community grudges, and motivation to seek revenge (Wiley, 2002). Reflecting on our understanding of original sin, Wiley's book revisited the exegesis of the Genesis story that until the renaissance centered on original sin as the result of a single event in history as described in the Yahwist account in Genesis. However, the renaissance humanists brought to biblical interpretation new critical methods. For example, Pascal (d. 1662) based his reflections on humanity in the present moment as simply "not complete and harmonious but divided within and burdened by contradictions, capable of self-transcendence but also degradation, a being both great and wretched" (p. 109).

Rahner (1975) said that a further complication is that present-day humans have come to believe that they are good as they are, sound, and whole. For them, original sin is simply identical to the absurdity of human existence and the finite nature of human beings (p. 1148). However, "original sin is certainly a mystery which is not to be rationally disintegrated" (p. 1150). He asserted that humans lack the sanctifying Holy Spirit but "the will of God is that man should have the divinizing Pneuma" (p. 1152). Yet, he said, the ability to respond to that intent of God depends on a moral decision for or against God (p. 1154).

If Original Sin is not a single event with inadequate explanations for its ongoing transmission but an ongoing process in time, then the processes of psychology and society as expounded by learning theory and motivation studies, are important to our understanding of how to do our human part to assist in repairing our condition.

The Wisdom/lay tradition immerses all its narratives and stories of the OT, NT, and church history periods squarely within the social fabric of society and historical community dilemma that replicate the concerns of theologians, old and new, who described original sin. Matthews (2008) wrote that the wisdom literature illustrates the concerns of the original sin theorists: our darkened understanding, weakened will, inclination toward evil, and the death and dying all around us. He continued that the wisdom literature adds concrete instances of honorable and shameful behavior, potential and actual disputes, and the bonds of kinship and identity. Additionally, the wisdom stories old and new contain social dislocations, everything from war to famine and exile. The wisdom narratives include obligations balanced and distorted, plus rural stories and city stories.

The key element here is that in the OT wisdom stories we recognize these social forces are ever-present with us today. Most importantly, the social connections and interactions in the OT and

NT wisdom parables and stories help explain how the effects of what was called original sin have been passed on in history and continue to be passed on.

Into this cauldron of human behavior and suffering, the ACT, acceptance, and commitment to action, model aims to increase flexibility in problem-solving, reduce cognitive confusion, confront avoidance, and provide a mental health bulwark against the pressures of social expectations. Without help such as the ACT processes, avoidance and confused actions emerge and gradually dominate in a person's repertoire that is detached from long-term desired qualities of living. Behavioral repertoires narrow and become less sensitive to the current context as it affords valued actions. Persistence and change in the service of effectiveness are less likely. (Hayes S. , Theory of Psychopathology).

Research shows that ACT methods are beneficial for a broad range of clients. ACT teaches clients and therapists alike how to alter the way difficult private experiences function mentally rather than having to eliminate them from occurring at all. This empowering message has been shown to help clients cope with a wide variety of clinical problems, including depression, anxiety, stress, substance abuse, and even psychotic symptoms. The benefits are as important for the clinician as they are for clients. Research shows that ACT quickly alleviates therapist burnout. In addition, we are learning that these same processes help us understand and change a variety of other behavioral problems, including human prejudice, work performance, or the inability to learn new things.

Our task in the parables and a goal of CPA is to assist in both neutralizing parts of the effects of our human condition and in supporting efforts to live happily while deciding firmly for God.

Reviewing our stories is intended to help us grow in our faith, and to commit or recommit us to post-baptismal formation. This life-long period, called mystagogy (RCIA #244), directs us to:

1. become "renewed in mind,

2. taste more deeply the sweetness of God's word,

3. receive the fellowship of the Holy Spirit, and

4. experience the goodness of the Lord" to "derive a new perception of the faith, of the Church, and the world" (RCIA #245).

Perhaps because Jesus' parables offer examples of both cognitive and behavioral competencies, they are ideal models for spiritual and psychological formation for therapists and clients.

Have you had an experience or personal observation that you feel moved to witness?

a. What was good about it?

b. What was bad about it?

c. How was God present for you in it?

Figure 15

Prayer is essential.

James Jasper

15

DISCERNMENT WITHIN PRAYER

Who is God-for-you when you pray?

Keating (1994, 2009, p. 22) wrote that our attitude toward God can reflect unconscious attitudes rooted in experiences of an angry father figure, a suspicious police officer, or a harsh judge in our past. Instead, Jesus in these parables calls for a complete reversal of those distortions. God calls us to grow in trust, our old wounds healed, and our unconscious motivations transformed and purified.

Jesus certainly encouraged extreme confidence in God's generosity and inclination to come to our aid. We have only to ask, seek, and knock in prayer to receive all sorts of good gifts from our heavenly Father (Matthew 7:7-11). Only if we approach God in shameless openness can we cut through the covert guilt and shame of admitting our biases, blindness, and experiential avoidance. This is Jesus' teaching on prayer.

Jesus shared three prayer parables. The three present images of God so socially challenging and paradoxical that if Jesus had not told them we would think the storyteller an adversary. The first two are similar in their challenge. For example, the parable of **a neighbor asleep and reluctant to get up,** (Mt. 7:7-11) encourages patience even when God seems to not be acting on our behalf—or is even too lazy to get out of bed to help us!

Our waiting does not change God's intention toward us but can shape our intention toward God's ways. Prayer shapes us even when it seems 'Do not bother me; the door has already been locked and my children and I are already in bed. I cannot get up to give you anything.' In those moments it can be tempting to repeat our requests over and over and hard to not think our persistence is what moves God, "I tell you, if he does not get up to give him the loaves because of their friendship, he will get up to give him whatever he needs because of his persistence" (Lk 11:5-13).

However, Jesus dissuaded us from repeating words. "In praying, do not babble like the pagans, who think that they will be heard because of their many words. Do not be like them. Your Father knows what you need before you ask him" (Matthew 6:7-8).

Put otherwise, just because we are waiting for the Lord to act does not mean we should fill the time with babbling! Instead, we might aim to rest in the Lord in contemplative prayer.

That is, our persistence and waiting must guide us to persevering in ever-increasing trust in the Lord. The scholars assert that the point of these two parables, **neighbor asleep and reluctant to get up,** (Mt. 7:7-11), is the "How much more?" Namely, God will respond so much more than a neighbor could or would. As Jesus asserted, it is in God's character to respond to our requests" (Snodgrass, 2018, p. 448). God is so much more than the best of neighbors, and waiting in trust "unveils" and expands our expectations of God's concern and generosity toward us.

However, Jesus challenges our personal view of God as an unjust judge or as someone asleep at his job. Instead, the point of Jesus' parables is that we should pray and expect a reward precisely when we feel or believe God is asleep, unjust, or a thief.

Instead, Jesus again asks how much more will his Father not act on our behalf, answer us, and bring them justice?

The parable of **the unjust judge** (Luke 18:1-8) follows a similar pattern. The issue here is to remain in trusting faith that Jesus' Father hears us and will act on our behalf. Like the parable of the sleeping neighbor, this is not a parable about badgering God. Instead, it asks for faith and trust that if we are patient God will vindicate our rights as he did for the widow (Blomberg, 2012, p. 461).

So, this third parable again asked how much more will your Heavenly Father respond to your needs? "It is hard for many people to imagine that it is appropriate to address God as an intimate friend, and Abba-father. It is harder still for most to think of praying with chutzpah or moxie, even though this is what we repeatedly see biblical believers doing, especially in Job, and the psalms of lament and imprecation. God can manage our gumption! Better to take out one's frustration with a fervent, direct prayer to God, especially for unanswered yet righteous requests, than to redirect it against fellow humans (Blomberg, 2012, pp. 378-379).

The fourth parable, **the pharisee and the tax collector** (Luke 18:10-14), also asks "How much more?" But in this case, the issue is authenticity in prayer. Remember that the Pharisee assumed his position and spoke this prayer to himself, "O God, I thank you that I am not like the rest of humanity—greedy, dishonest, adulterous—or even like this tax collector. I fast twice a week, and I pay tithes on my whole income." The pharisee had respectable, legalistic righteousness. God rejected the presumed righteousness.

The tax collector had a "received righteousness" acceptable to God because neither the tax collector nor any of us can produce the perfect righteousness required for life with God without the power of the Holy Spirit (Kendall, 2004, 2006, pp. 310-312).

Jesus' response was to say that the tax collector went home justified but the Pharisee did not. It was a perfect example of someone who did the socially acceptable repentance elements: fasting and almsgiving but since he enlarged his public self, God humbled him, and the tax collector who humbled himself, God praised (Luke 18:10-14). It is an illustration of Jesus' principle, "(1) Those who exalt themselves will be humbled and (2) Those who humble themselves will be exalted." The key insight is that this will apply at the last judgment but has countless applications at any moment before our final judgment.

This is a reversal parable. The pharisee had performed all the legal prescriptions for forgiveness but was not. The tax collector did none of that but was. Soren Kierkegaard's sermon on this is that when we are alone with God and look up, we realize how wretched we are and how rightly fearful we are that without God's help we are in peril. The Pharisee looked down, saw that all was in order, that he was respectable and legally correct, so his egoism was socially acceptable but rejected by God. That is, God's judgment is diametrically distinct from ours (Snodgrass, 2018, p. 475).

Yet from a discernment perspective, the attitudes of these four prayer parables can be problematic for the spirituality of even the visibly devout. As Keating (2006, pp. 140-157) wrote, since the enlightenment of the 18th century, the Western model of spirituality has stressed these attitudes:

1. <u>External acts are more important than internal acts</u>. "External acts" refer to rituals, good works, fasting, almsgiving, and bodily penances. "Internal acts" refers to the motives these actions spring from and they can come from pride and self-centeredness as easily as from love of God and respect for others. Jesus is clear, "Clean the inside of the cup first and then worry about the outside."

2. <u>The self initiates all good works and God rewards them</u>. This is heresy, the Pelagian heresy. God does not sit back and wait for us to decide. In the gospel, God initiated all action within us by the power and prompting of the Spirit.

3. <u>The greatest concern is getting to heaven by doing good and required actions, such as the sacraments</u>. This attitude led to a neglect of the needs of the poor in the here and now as well as ignorance that when St. Paul spoke of the Body of Christ, he was in line with Jesus who came to save not just individuals but the whole earth with all its citizens.

In each of these four parables, Jesus urges us to have clarity in our understanding of God and sincerity in our values. Lack of clarity in values even in prayer demands discernment in our understanding of who God is relative to us. Outer appearances do not equal God's evaluation.

The ACT approach to psychotherapy stresses a parallel psychological approach to lack of clarity regarding true holiness. The ACT approach focuses on individual personal meaningful paths and directions that lead to a rich and fulfilling life. While the ACT Core Process in no way supplants Jesus' spiritual instruction, clients defining their valued direction versus aimlessness can support a turn from lack of values, confusion of goals with values, and other values problems. ACT can also contribute to building broad and flexible repertoires for reassessing our implicit human and Christian values.

Jesus told parables to motivate and reflecting on our stories can help us "tune in" to that motivation. The rule in motivation psychology is that if we did something we did it because we were motivated to do it. Conversely, if you did not do something, it was because you were not motivated to do it. If we wish we could pray or act more Christ-like, but do not seem to be able to, the answer to your "stuckness" is in your story. Listen for it and ask God to help you become "unstuck."

Thus, if your prayer feels "stuck" or pointless it could be that you view God as a

<ul style="list-style:none">
<li>a. Police officer</li>
<li>b. Judge</li>
<li>c. Busy manager</li>
<li>d. Toll collector</li>
<li>e. Bank manager</li>
<li>f. Or in other limited human terms.</li>
</ul>

When we say, "let us pray," we may think of a particular prayer practice. However, we are saying "let us have a relationship with God," or "let us continue the one we already have," or "let us be open to a still deeper relationship."

Psalms are the book in the wisdom literature we most frequently hear in the readings at Mass. The psalms influence every aspect of the spirituality of the Church and religious communities.

Tucker (2008) pointed to poetic devices such as repetition as saying the same truth forwards and backward and repeating a line at the beginning and end of a psalm. The aesthetics of the psalms (Brueggemann, 1985) nourish and nurture through patterns of orientation, disorientation, and a new orientation to expand and reorient our perspectives on God, others, and life. Viewed as a whole (Tucker, 2008) the psalms present God as king, creator, refuge, and victor over all enemies.

Praying the psalms regularly fosters a relationship with God through a process of growing intimacy. Viewed as a relationship, Christian prayer is rooted in the word of God in scripture and the person of Jesus Christ. Keating (1994, 2009) wrote that in his Word God intends to convince us of his unconditional love in taking the initiative with us. Our relationship with God grows just as human relationships grow from formal introduction to more informal friendliness, to self-disclosing and committed friendship, and ideally toward union of life in the intimacy of a shared life.

As we read God's word in the parables, we experience an introduction to God's perspective. If we reflect on Jesus' perspective and respond with faith, hope, and love, we begin to assimilate and live in and with God in joy and peace. Reading and reflecting on God's word is a four-step process, namely, the four "R"s: read, reflect, respond, and rest.

We may think of prayer as thoughts or feelings expressed in words such as vocal prayer, reflective prayer, and spontaneous prayer. These are not the only expressions of prayer.

Instead, the Gospel asks us to allow the Holy Spirit to transform us here and now and to give, not simply good behavior, but our inner selves to God. God's perspective is of a process toward growth in friendship with us. The Holy Spirit powers that relationship with us whenever we allow the Spirit to transform us.

God always builds on our here-and-now experiences and opportunities to do two things. First, the Spirit is always present to tear down any avoidance and destruction of our relationships with God and others. Second, the Spirit is always present to turn us to God and others more fully in love.

Our task is to listen, to open our hearts, and to develop our sensitivity and strength in responding to the subtle promptings of the Spirit. In that context, prayer at its best is a subtle response.

How has God worked in prayer with your strengths, your weaknesses, and been with you in crucial moments or provided what you needed in that time?

      a. What was good about it?

      b. What was bad about it?

      c. How was God present for you in it?

Figure 16

Money and values.

James Jasper

16

MONEY AND PRIORITIES

Two ACT processes can help us clarify and prioritize values. For example, we might desire greater resistance to consumerist blindness. The ACT processes of helping clients to clarify their values and then helping them find ways of acting on those values, (Hayes, Strosahl, & Wilson, 2012) can even work for those who consciously or unconsciously operate from a value system proclaiming, "Let's make lots of money." ACT can remind them of Jesus' view of consumerist greed. Such clarification means that the person's faith can grow on a meaningful path through life that leads to a richer and more fulfilling life.

This ACT focus emphasizes that it is not enough to consider the behavior of the individual, we must consider social context as well (Hankle, 2013, p. 23). For CPA clinical members, OT proverbs and NT Catholic letters offer strategies for those aspiring to live as Christians in the world.

Jesus' parables demonstrate contextual awareness linked to competent, praxis. ACT's functional contextual psychology is a kind of case study approach to developing competence in CPA terms. Long (2018, pp. 17-27) linked pragmatism and contextualism to praxis, a most useful standard for psychotherapists.

Long wrote of William James' emphasis on praxis as a concrete way of thinking that has an applied social element (p. 18). It "strives for a coherent, holistic, organic, and evolutionary model of justification and discovery" (p. 19). In his view, contextual competence starts from the subjective. For Long, William James was a good philosopher because James was a real human person" (p. 33) willing to share his subjective life experience.

The Biblical Story

The parable of **the dishonest or unjust steward/manager** (Luke 16:1-13) "has always been difficult to interpret and to link up with its context in the bible" (Harrington, 1969, p. 1012).

Blomberg (2012, p. 325) concisely summarized the main points of the parable, namely, that "1) All of God's people will be called to give a reckoning of the nature of their service to him. 2) Preparation for that reckoning should involve a prudent, shrewd use of all our resources, especially in finances. 3) Such prudence and shrewdness demonstrating a life of true discipleship, will be rewarded with eternal life and joy." These three key points are certainly the parable's intent in forming our attitudes toward money. Jesus referred to such financial wealth as mammon, or wealth regarded as an evil influence, as covetousness, or as a false object of adoration and affection.

Snodgrass (2018, pp. 417-418) wrote that scholars struggle with this parable even though the behavior of the dishonest or unjust manager was the customary practice of writing down debt to escape prison or worse when legal bankruptcy was not an option. Snodgrass gave examples of biblical commentators tying themselves in knots to explain this parable. How can the owner commend the dishonest manager for stealing from him? Was the master condoning theft?

One way of applying this parable of the dishonest steward of the master's goods is to point out that the steward/manager wrote down the master's receivables not his own. Might I point out that in parishes we can see this pattern all the time? People who want to make up for their shortcomings aim to pay down the receivables owed to God by contributing to the parish or another charity in the form of almsgiving.

That is, in a spirit of penance and almsgiving we can each acknowledge that we owe a debt to God. However, it is impossible to repay anything to the Lord of the Universe who created all that is. So, in response, we perceive that by redirecting a percentage-tithe of our income in almsgiving to someone in need we reduce our debts to God in the well-founded principle that because we did it for someone in need Jesus proclaims we do it for Him.

In psychoanalytic terms, the manager's behavior was "undoing," a defense mechanism by which individuals attempt to avoid intended consequences by "making un-happen" past behavior and impulses, even if only at a symbolic level. Christian strategies to match the unjust manager's undoing behavior can be found in the NT wisdom literature, namely, the Catholic letters.

Discernment regarding money can begin by noticing that it has always been true that people focused on getting rich consider themselves wiser than Christians. However, that financial "wisdom" in each age is the wisdom of the present world. By comparison, Christians prioritize not just turning a financial profit, but also considering how our stewardship will look when we appear before God. There is an urgency to the responsibility for the needy, the little ones, here and now. Also, how will we answer for the use of our time and talent later in the there and then? This parable does not say how we are to balance the here-and-now versus the there-and-then when we will appear before God. However, Jesus' parable directs us to do our best to be prudent in balancing our responses to the needy today with an eye to our hope of one day appearing irreproachable before Jesus (Colossians 1:22).

Commentators as well as people with worldly ideas dismiss the steward's behavior as theft by the manager and as having no place in their understanding of money and finance. The interpretation I have heard too often begins with something such as, "That's all well and good, but now let's get real and talk money." Such a monetary or consumerist bias, as Hardin wrote (2020, p. xviii), tends to distort all aspects of Cristian belief, the crucifixion, resurrection, and afterlife to meet consumerist expectations. They expect Christianity for them to meet their "every whim, wish, and desire," like a trip to the mall.

In contrast, Jesus' cautioned us, "Take care to guard against all greed, for though one may be rich, one's life does not consist of possessions" (Luke 12:15). To exercise Christian discernment, we must ask God to "unveil" our consumerist blindness. In that unveiling, Jesus advocated for almsgiving (Matthew 6:3) both to free us from consumerist greed and to help meet the needs of the poor.

In our stories, we do well to pay attention to Jesus' methodology in telling his stories. In Jesus' case, he was asked 183 questions, answered only 3, and, in turn, commented and asked 307 return questions (Copenhaver, 2014). Many of the gospel and other biblical parables are unexpected and surprising responses to either-or questions asked. However, instead of choosing either one option or another Jesus responds with remarkable flexibility to use images to bring listeners from the abstract there-and-then to their here-and-now life experiences.

Rohr called Jesus' approach (2001, 2020), order, disorder, reorder. It is an approach common to biblical Wisdom literature and familiar to any storyteller. For example, in AA (Alcoholics Anonymous), recovering people tell their stories over and over and in their storytelling make progressive approximations to the truth and complexity of their lives.

Spirituality for a material world requires being in the present moment and its concrete realities (Hankle, 2013, p. 24). Attending to our concrete realities is an endless necessity and can open us to God's judgment and wisdom in the present moment. In support of that effort, parables are discrete stories with countless applications. Parables facilitate praxis, that is, in-depth learning and practical application of specific skills, techniques, and approaches in the practice of psychotherapy.

Further, ACT emphasizes workability as a truth criterion. That is, in psychotherapy an approach must be practicable or feasible. In my experience, the growing number of ACT workbooks demonstrated to me the practical workability of the ACT perspective where thoughts and feelings do not cause other actions, except as regulated by context.

Helping clients to clarify their values, to consider if those values will lead them where they hope, and then act assertively on their values is both an ACT goal and a valuable process for those aiming to live Christian values. Pulling those things together is praxis.

Praxis is the process by which an action embodies or realizes a theory, lesson, or skill. "Praxis" may also refer to the act of engaging, applying, exercising, realizing, or practicing ideas. The parables accomplish that.

In considering our life story, has there ever been a time where you have exercised psychoanalytic undoing through almsgiving to a needy cause?

    a. What was good about that?

    b. What was bad about that?

    c. How was God present for you in it?

Figure 17

The fruitful tree.

James Jasper

17

BEARING GOOD FRUIT

In the search for a fruitful rather than a futile life, ACT's emphasis on acceptance of reality can motivate therapists and clients to confront the avoidance of the implications of judgment in evaluating our fruitfulness as Christian individuals and groups. This is especially significant for those living in secular cultures and subcultures that reject God, the owner of the vineyard.

A secular model for this is the zero-sum game. That is, a situation in game theory in which one person's gain is equivalent to another's loss, so the net change in wealth or benefit is zero but where the emphasis or attention or focus definitively shifts.

Rather than an abstract image such as game theory, the wisdom literature, and Jesus' stories use images of life (Pokrifa, 2008). Specifically, Jesus and the wisdom literature speak of the breath of life given to animals. However, an even simpler example is the image of a plant or tree such as the fruit tree by streams of water (Psalm 1:3; Proverbs 1:7, 9:10, 15:33).

The wisdom literature imagines the futile life as chaff (Psalm 1:4, 83:13) or, even worse, a fig tree that looks like a healthy tree but bears no fruit.

Four of Jesus' parables use fig trees to illustrate **the necessity of bearing the fruit of justice**. They are challenges to individual believers and the Church to bear fruit or risk the consequences.

The first fig tree describes a **barren tree** (Luke 13:6-9) that had failed over three years to produce fruit. The fig tree denied the owner, God, any fruit for three years. In the parable, the owner, God, told the gardener to cut the tree down if it did not bear fruit in the future. That is a warning to all that failure to produce the fruit of justice leads to fatal spiritual consequences.

In Matthew (21:19-20) Jesus **cursed a fig tree** that had leaves, but no fruit. The tree immediately withered. Thus, even if we delay thinking about God's judgment for failing to produce fruits of judgment and mercy the consequences for not being fruitful or productive are a cause for judgment (Snodgrass, 2018, p. 265). The application can easily apply to both individuals and the whole Church past, present, and future.

However, Keating (1994, 2009) stressed "fruit" in the Christian Scriptures is not initiating projects but on listening and responding to the Spirit. Put in parallel terms, God calls us to holiness in the circumstances of our own lives and the Spirit can make us holy in the circumstances of our lives. It is a concept that parallels the ACT principles of contextualism. Thus, a CPA therapist can use psychological principles to help clients identify the contextual situations where God's holiness can find a place in us.

The **wicked tenant-farmers** (Luke 20:9:19) is a most significant parable (Snodgrass p. 282-298) in that "For some, the parable says too much for them to be comfortable that it represents the view of Jesus." "The stakes (of the parable) are high, for, unlike most parables, this one is of direct and major significance." In the parable, the tenants beat the servants of God, and sent them away empty, wounded, and cast out. The servants are the prophets, and the son and heir is Jesus crucified and murdered by the tenants. This parable is salvation history on a grand scale (p. 284).

The evil tenant-farmers, the religious authorities "…realized that this parable was aimed at them, but they were afraid of the people" (Lk. 20:19). This parable is allegorical in that elements correspond to salvation history Bock (2012, p. 292). It is also a warning to all that the kingdom of God and his son are brimming with boundless prospects but also with vast demands. When we read it, we may find our reaction similar to those of many ages past: the opportunities are welcome but the judgment involved tends to be avoided.

A second story centered on how a fig tree grows and develops **the lesson of the fig tree** (Luke 21:29–31) which stresses that when its buds emerge, we see for ourselves that summer is upon us. Then we wonder what the summer will bring.

The emphasis in the second fig tree parable is the nearness of God's judgment. All evidence of a fig tree sprouting leaves will pass with the season. Then the leaves will fall to the ground. Thus, no generation can avoid God's judgment of their productivity.

So, where can we turn for a sure guide? In the next sentence, Jesus assured us that heaven, earth, and the physical universe will pass away, but his words will not pass away. There is safety and salvation in following his words. It follows that such practices as sacred reading, *Lectio Divina*, can be a life-saver available to all. In our case, Jesus' parables and even our stories can dispose us to "hear" Jesus' words and let them lead and enlighten us.

The parables anchor discernment in concrete and immediate terms (Hankle, 2013, p. 16). For example, Jesus used the process of a fig tree's growth as a symbol of a wise person reading "the signs of the times" which is as sure as the process of a fig tree growing. Buds emerge in spring, then leaves, and finally fruit. In each chapter, I have provided signs of the times that I suspect apply to Jesus' words. Does your discerning judgment pick up on similar signs?

St. Paul's list of the fruits of the work of the Holy Spirit in us includes love, joy, peace, patience, kindness, generosity, faithfulness, gentleness, and self-control (Galatians 5:22-23a). This list is one illustration of the good fruit Jesus had in mind.

Conversely, what is the process of people and groups drifting to evil? The importance of truth in producing true or false prophets and disciples is in Jesus' fourth reflection on good and bad fruit in a section cautioning his followers about **true versus false prophets** (Matthew 7:15-20). He stressed we should not judge by appearances because false prophets come in sheep's clothing but internally are like voracious wolves. However, if we are to discern we should look to their fruits. True prophets will produce good fruit and false prophets are incapable of anything but bad fruits.

Thus, while we cannot see the interior life of people, we can have some sense of others' interior cognitions and motivations by their "fruits" or lack thereof. That exterior observation is imperfect just as psychological assessment is always imperfect. However, it is what we must work with. It is imperfect but is still valuable.

To repeat, please discern that parables intend to motivate. ACT offers two skill sets that can increase our positive motivations and decrease our negative motivations. Two of the ACT processes require that we reshuffle our values, priorities, and observe our actual behaviors dispassionately.

I encourage therapists to consider and try any of the ACT workbooks to discover if they work as well for them as they did for me. Alternatively, therapists may find it more helpful to seek out one of many ACT training available.

The first of these pivotal ACT skillsets is called reducing our *attachment to a conceptualized self*. This skill set entails, for example, experiencing self-as-context (Trueman, 2020) and getting real about money in the context of now and later. ACT workbooks on this skill set stress a sense of self that transcends immediate experiences. The aim is a "you" that can observe and experience your inner and outer world so that you are more than your thinking, feeling, and acting.

The second pivotal ACT skillset refers to the *dominance of the conceptualized past and feared future (economics vs. trust)*. For many people trusting self, others, and God are major tasks. For others, letting go of depressing past events (Strosahl & Robinson, 2017) or anxieties about the future are major psychotherapeutic tasks (Forsyth & Eifert, 2016). For yet a third group, developing present-moment awareness and contemplative prayer is a long-term process in prayer (Keating, 2006).

The opposite of a barren fig tree is a fig tree bearing fruit. Thus, we counter relativism and scientism and find the certitude and values that could assist in discernment by following the Spirit of Jesus. We assess our progress by measuring the quality of our work against the behavioral qualities of the fruits of the Spirit. Therefore, resolve to go wherever the Word and the Spirit lead us.

Discernment is a process. Our task is first learning and practicing what Jesus directs us to and avoiding what he forbids us from. If we love God, we keep God's commandments (John 14:15). Our disposition in this needs to be openness to whatever God wants. The means for learning and practicing for Catholic Christians can include a variety of spiritual "exercises" or practices such as Eucharist, reading the Bible, silence, spiritual direction, or review of spiritual experience.

The power of exposing ourselves to the Word of God to turn us into discerning, that is, true disciples is illustrated by Jesus' short parable on **the seed growing of itself** (Mark 4:26-29). Jesus observed that after someone scatters seed, of its own accord the plant grows bit by bit itself until it is harvest time. The growing of the effects of the Word of God, once planted in our consciousness, is also an unstoppable process unless we interfere with that growth.

How are the 12 fruits manifested qualitatively and behaviorally in your life? For example, do you look to the qualitative and behavioral evidence of charity (or love), joy, peace, patience, benignity (or kindness), goodness, longanimity (or long-suffering), mildness (or gentleness), faith, modesty, continency (or self-control), and chastity?

Attending to our stories helps us develop psychological and spiritual health like a tree growing in which leaves change but the core remains. We need to learn how to read that growth in us.

Do you have an incident or a moment in your life where you reflected on the fruit or results of your efforts to understand yourself, to serve others, or to respond to God?

    a. What was good about it?

    b. What was bad about it?

    c. How was God present for you in it?

Figure 18

Escaping futility.

James Jasper

18

FROM FUTILITY TO TRANSFORMATION

When we say that **grace transforms nature**, we can then say that psychotherapy helps to clear away in this life all the detritus of evildoing in the world and individuals. Thus, the fruit of Catholic psychotherapy is spiritual and psychological makeovers that aspire to the good fruit of internal transformation and care for those in psychological or social systems distress.

To turn the image of the fig tree into an analogy, the priestly/apostolic tradition is like the visible branches providing structure and continuity in visible growth. The roots are like the prophetic tradition, at times almost invisible (1 Samuel 3:1-3; Deuteronomy 34:10), but bigger than the visible tree, and nourishing all above. The leaves are like the wisdom/lay tradition that blossoms anew in every age. In this image, Jesus is the trunk holding all together. However, all must work together to produce fruit. If any part is absent or injured the result is futile growth.

The parable of Dives, the rich man, and Lazarus, the poor man illustrates the daily and eternal perspectives in concrete and immediate terms.

Blomberg (2012, p. 259) summarized the key points of the parable. Namely, that 1) like Lazarus, those whom God helps will be borne after their death into God's presence. 2) Like the rich man, the unrepentant will experience irreversible punishment. In the rich man's case, his miserliness was his undoing. 3) Through Abraham, Moses, and the prophets (and now through Jesus), God reveals himself and his will so that none who neglect it can legitimately protest their subsequent fate.

In this story note how Jesus moved effortlessly from earth to heaven and hell. Plus, he linked earthly behavior to the proportionality of other-worldly life. In the telling it is all so self-evident, locking us in rational empathy. Plus, Abraham, as God's vicar, consoles the poor man. Also, remarkably, the rich man, even in hell, has the same attitude, "Eh, Abraham, send that poor man to get a drop of water to relieve my torment!' It is such an immovable attitude of entitlement. In this story, the world's false priorities are jarringly illustrated in the reality of heaven in Abraham's bosom and the rich man in torment.

Also, the dialogue at the end convinced the greedy and unempathetically abusive rich man that the true nature of heaven and hell had to be proclaimed to his brothers.

Abraham's last line most dramatically summarized Jesus' experience that even when he rose from the dead, as he did, others did not believe.

Jesus' observation parallels William James' observation that actual religious experiences always convince the person but seldom convince anyone else. That is because experiences are not transferrable. Each person typically has to experience a reality for themselves!

However, the rich man's sense of entitlement and superiority is evident in presuming that the poor man should run and get a drop of water for him. In the end, we are left with a sense of the vast and unalterable distance between the final location of the rich man and the poor man.

The Yahwist, the Bible's first theologian is a model of discernment. The Yahwist name derives from the author's reference to God as Yahweh. Scholars trace the Yahwist influence throughout Genesis. The Yahwist wrote 800 years after the patriarchs (Ellis, 1968, pp. 42-44), in the era of David and Solomon. The Yahwist intended to "teach his audience about Yahweh, the Lord of history, about the meaning of Israel's history, and themselves as individuals and as God's covenanted people" (p. 43).

By literature type Genesis resembles a saga, a form of the novel in which the members or generations of a family or social group are chronicled in a long narrative. In that saga, the first figure is Adam meaning "son of the red Earth," a name that refers to the reddish color associated with human skin. In our common jargon, a better equivalent suggested by Scott Hahn is simply "Humanity" (Hahn, 2002, p. 4).

If we treat the early chapters of Genesis as theology rather than literal history, then we see past the inspired author's figurative language and use of imagery to trace the history of humanity's struggles back through our ancient history (Catechism #390). The Yahwist used images where we might use theological terms. However, the theme reflects humanity's history and current condition. Original sin (National Conference of Catholic Bishops, 2006) is a conception developed in centuries past when the history of humanity was understood to be a few thousand years in length rather than the millions of years of humanity's development on earth (Burton, 2011). However, whether in the saga in Genesis or anthropological research humanity's condition is out of harmony with the world and with one another and in need of God's help (Catechism #388).

From today's perspective, Original Sin is not a single event with inadequate explanations for its ongoing transmission (Wiley, 2002). Rather, it is an all too real ongoing process in time, both the distant past and the current state of humanity. From that perspective, the processes of psychology and society as demonstrated in learning theory and motivation studies, as well as the reparative power of psychotherapy are important to our understanding of how to assist in repairing our condition.

The OT adapted to shifts in the human condition through a process called hermeneutics (Goldingay, 2008, pp. 267-277). That is a term that means literally to translate. However, as human history shifted so did the Bible's response to history, culture, to our poverty or riches, or our male and female sexuality. For example, after the exile, life was difficult for the Judean community.

Ezra and Nehemiah used the stories of Esther and Daniel as models of living in spiritual freedom during extremely difficult political times. Goldingay added that each book of the Bible gives clues on how to interpret what is written from the perspective of who was the ruler, what the era was like, and the concerns of the day. Adjustments included new liturgical interpretations, devotional innovations, insertion of prophetic experiences testifying to the living God, fresh narrative styles, timely updates, and even feminist interpretations (Judith, Esther, Sarah, and Mary).

The habit of working to increase good fruit is called virtue. That is, doing our part to counter the effects of the human condition. For the Catholic psychotherapist and any client or person, the desired outcomes are virtue and competence. In *After Virtue* (MacIntyre, 1981, 1984, 2007) maintained that virtue has evaporated in the loss of objective goals. However, accepting the reality of the two realms in the rich man/poor man parable focuses us on preparing for life with God.

It was Aristotle's key idea that virtues are habits. Virtue is the foundation for holiness. The theological or "God" virtues inform our relationship with God through faith, hope, and love. Competence, in other traditions known as discernment, informs our clinical judgment of others as expressed in the central, also known as cardinal virtues of prudence, justice, fortitude, and temperance.

Cessario, Titus, and Vitz's (2013) book is a praiseworthy reframing of the operational definitions of virtue in our time with attention to its therapeutic applications. In their telling, the three theological virtues-faith, hope, and charity—with the four traditional cardinal virtues—prudence, justice, fortitude, temperance—deserve and get a thorough update in current psychological and philosophical terms. At the very least their update is a refreshing and enlightening conversation starter on the renewal of the philosophy of virtue.

Aristotle's expanded philosophy of virtue spoke to his day, but Cessario, Titus, and Vitz's work more nearly reflect ours. They offer several categories of virtue that deserve further study and will, hopefully, function as conversation starters in virtue philosophy. Their list of virtues includes:

1. Psychotherapy
2. "Personal unity"
3. "Ordered inclinations"
4. Reasonable acts
5. Free choices
6. Balanced emotions
7. Poised strength
8. Tempered desire.

The net result of this discussion is that our understanding of "original sin" is morphing into a developmental human condition filled with human weakness and sin that Catholic theology describes so well. However, what is new is that Catholic psychotherapy has an emerging role in laying the groundwork and building a foundation for holiness, and assisting in God's grace in transforming nature.

Like our stories that are sometimes complicated, God's revelation to humanity is paradoxical. That is, to be truly human we must be more spiritual. Conversely, to be truly spiritual we must be more human. That has been a theme in my religious experiences in that the loftier and more mystical the experiences are, unexpectedly, the more human and truly myself I experience being me.

Hankle (2013, p. 18) points out that **Christian anthropology views us as embodied spirits, created by God, retuning to God, and here gifted with sexuality as the essential truth of humanity.**

Does this parable lead you to reflect in human and concrete terms what effects your actions will produce both now and later?

    a. What was good about it?

    b. What was bad about it?

    c. How was God present for you in it?

Figure 19

Sheep or goats?

James Jasper

19

THE BANQUET ON THE LORD'S MOUNTAIN

In contrast to scientism and relativism, **God's plan for us can be summed up in one word, "Dinner!"**

Parables are all about using visible things as signs of the invisible and reflecting on the observable to help us with the invisible. From a psychotherapeutic perspective, we work with clients' thoughts, feelings, and actions (T-F-A) to reach the spiritual and religious.

In this vein, Pope Benedict XVI (2006) distinguished science from scientism. Science is an activity that seeks to explore the natural world using well-established, clearly-delineated methods. Science expands our understanding, rather than limiting it. Scientism, on the other hand, is a speculative worldview about the ultimate reality of the universe and its meaning, that maintains that science is the sum of all knowledge.

The result has been that all knowledge is viewed as relative and that a scientific worldview precludes all that is spiritual or unable to be measured by the scientific method. The impact this has had on virtue and faith formation is my focus here. Hopefully, our reflections on the biblical proverbs and analogies here will provide renewed approaches to discernment in faith, motivation toward virtue, and formation prospects. As a result, a work such as this is essential in linking our Catholic faith experience to valid advances in empirically validated science.

The great feast (Lk. 14:15-24) parable emphasizes that God generously and consistently invites all kinds of people into his kingdom but that a day will come when the invitation is canceled, and it is too late to respond. Yet from the excuses of the first group of guests stems the principle that all excuses for rejecting God's invitation are exceedingly lame. However, God's generosity is not thwarted by the rejection of the 'establishment,' because he extends his invitation even to the dispossessed of this world (Blomberg, 2012, p. 307).

In Matthew (22:11) the dinner is a wedding banquet and includes a man not in the required wedding garment, a symbol of readiness for the new age (Jeremias, p. 115) in which all will be made new. As T. S. Eliot's adaptation of Julian of Norwich's words said, at that great wedding banquet "All shall be well, and all shall be well, and all manner of thing shall be well."

As we think about the biblical stories as well as our stories, we might return to two images the image of the mountains and the image of unveiling.

About the mountains... From a discernment perspective, within the lay/Wisdom tradition in images (Strawn, 2008) of "accompanying" travelers on their life journeys perhaps especially through and over mountains. Those journeys include

> ➢ campfires for millions of years

> ➢ biblical stories

> ➢ but now for 150 or so years psychotherapists as mountain guides and companions.

Mythic mountain imagery runs through all the wisdom tradition as images for God's lofty kingship (VanGemeren, 2008). The mountain images are also expressions of humanity's longing for discernment and wisdom as means of climbing high enough to see God's face in our human body (Job 19:26).

Digesting Jesus' parables, other stories in the Bible, and stories from our lives can offer us a path leading to a fruitful life that includes both virtue and competence. The parables can be looked at as examples of competent praxis. More specifically, "What does it mean for a person in ministry or psychotherapy to practice of the spiritual works of mercy, essential in the **judgment of the nations** (Matthew 25:31-46) where all pictured **sheep and**

goats are judged on their acts of mercy to the least of God's people. What is shocking to all in that judgment scene is how Jesus takes any actions toward the needy as done to and for him.

To apply discernment, a useful question can be, "What is it to be considered competent in applying/acting on/working within the context of this or that parable?" How can this parable be a guide through this client's journey? The answer is that parables can function as trails through awe-inspiring mountains. Even in a lifetime, we could never hike through all the mountains or even visit one single mountain in all its seasons.

However, bear in mind that since no two excursions are the same even if we follow the same pathways, no two stories are the same. However, the value of stories is that each one, if well told, is brief, illustrative, engaging, usually with a punch line, unique, and easily transported.

At the very least anyone who went camping in any of the Rockies or anywhere in the western mountains of the Americas could capture the sense of smallness and vulnerability the mountains foster. Therefore, bear in mind that none of us can do it all. Instead, we do well to humbly keep Jesus' words in mind "When you have done all you have been commanded, say, 'We are **unprofitable servants**; we have done what we were obliged to do.'" (Luke 17:10). Jesus does not say we are worthless but that no matter how much we are doing God is doing more. It is because we hope God will use our small contributions so that God's intent will be achieved.

About unveiling… We do well to remind ourselves of God's promise in Isaiah (25:7) "I will remove the veil that veils all people." Our efforts here are to link our prayers that God will remove our personal and social "veils" with the help of the guidance of the Word of God and perhaps with an assist from a series of ACT tools.

The goal of discernment is to understand how we are all created for God and that members of the community have a hand in helping everyone reach the goals God has in mind for us (Hankle, 2013, p. 24).

The goal of the book is to help us avoid becoming blind guides. We aim to unveil others' perceptions so that "Your word (Lord) is a lamp to my steps and a light to my path" (Ps. 119:105). William James was a contextualist whose approach to philosophy is the role of pathfinder, namely, "Pragmatists are philosophers who wander and 'who do not create anything beyond the marking of trail through the otherwise trackless forest of human experience'" (Long, 2018, p. 15).

In working on our stories, you have hopefully learned to make the expression of your story personal in the wisdom/lay tradition. The parables can be a foundation for discernment principles. Each chapter has worked to spell out one or another of the many discernment principles of the parables. Reflecting on them can be a means of developing the clinical and spiritual good judgment that is the mark of discernment.

An ongoing concern during the composition of this book has been the formation of CPA members. Our concern for our brothers and sisters absent from the Eucharistic table of the Lord is how to reach out to the 50% not involved. However, psychotherapists see them constantly and can help them to be more informed Catholic Christians.

Thus, this book aims to formulate a path for the ongoing formation of members in both the Christian identity and the appropriate professional skills of the Catholic psychotherapist. The parables offer praxis and mostly involve individuals with concrete analogies of short stories. They can be models for training Catholic psychotherapists who are present when clients are working out values. Also, the parables do not require the many years of study appropriate to the apostolic/priestly model or the extended life in a vowed community to be clear and demonstrative.

The parables are short jewels of instruction, a major part of Jesus' teaching, and endowed with God's power in instructing both therapists and anyone else who will hear them and ask God for help in understanding them.

In the interest of helping to make connections between psychotherapy resources and the resources of Catholic anthropology, I have introduced several skills and resources. Certainly, countless resources exist throughout God's creation, but this was enough for this work.

I realize that an introduction is not enough. However, perhaps your curiosity will be aroused enough to look up one or another resource that is new to you, to read about it, get some training in it if it is new to you, and bring what you have read or learned to your work with clients.

I also used as one possible worthwhile model Hayes, Strosahl, and Wilson's (2012) ACT processes. ACT is a current and worthwhile example of integrating, identifying, and working with interpersonal skills, and values with attention to clients' current environments. My contribution has been to suggest the need to connect psychotherapy with the necessity for:

- ✓ flexibility,
- ✓ seeing with ACT (Acceptance and Commitment Therapy) eyes,
- ✓ developing an ACT relationship,
- ✓ creating a context for change,
- ✓ remaining in the present moment,
- ✓ connecting with values and
- ✓ committing to action."

I hope that after reading this book readers will be able to:

1) Identify Hayes' (2012) seven mindful skills (1) flexibility, 2) seeing with ACT (Acceptance and Commitment Therapy) eyes, 3) developing an ACT relationship, 4) creating a context for change, 5) remaining in the present moment, 6) connecting with values, and 7) committing to action.)

2) Name at least one way in which Hayes' skills echo Jesus' approach to circumstances and people.

3) Find ways in which psychotherapy brings unique resources to therapist and client psychological and spiritual growth and development

Thus, this is one example drawn from the vast field of psychotherapy, motivation, learning theory, hundreds of models, but shows possibilities for one of these that is currently helpful. Psychotherapy evolves even as doctrine develops its understanding and practice shifts on the bedrock of creed, sacraments, life in Christ, and prayer.

The purpose of tracking our stories is to develop our discernment skills and remove some of our blindness.

St. John of the Cross has two images for this process. The first is that examining our life with God's help is like cleaning a very dirty window so the light can shine in. His second image spoke of throwing a green log into a blazing fire. The log first sizzles and gives off a lot of smoke before it can burn brightly.

Discerning is not just concern for the big decisions of life, that is, our major turning points. It also comes into play with the smallest of movements in the way we think, feel, and act moment to moment. A sign of our advancement in holiness is when we more and more frequently turn to the Spirit of Jesus to guide us in all things.

That turning to God is an unending task. Even when we are in God's city at the great banquet of the Lord, we will need to reflect on how best to comport ourselves in what we say, how we are feeling, and how we act. I have heard it said that the Holy Spirit is like a teacher coaxing us to sit up at dinner, pay attention to those around us, and consider what we want to say and how to listen to others. That is undoubtedly simplistic. However, it is never too soon to learn the fear of the Lord (Phil. 2:12), to learn discernment by asking for wisdom (1 Kings 3:1-15), and to learn all we can from Jesus "the way, the truth, and the life" (Jn. 14:6).

Jonah is two pages long, and about the length of a comics set at an open microphone. It is the work of a master storyteller presumably basing this parody on a few gripping historical facts that were known about Jonah 300-500 years after the prophet. The storyteller's approach is similar to the literary process that produced the Broadway play, *Hamilton*. The Broadway play is only modestly historical unless we maintain that the founding fathers spoke in rap, were racially integrated, and sang and danced together in their deliberations.

Whereas Elijah and Elisha came in the power and wonder-working of the Lord, Jonah is the anti-prophet who ran from God and distorted his commission from God to warn Nineveh by adding threats of destruction. Like all the wisdom literature the Jonah parable has elements of the sensational (Stuart D. , 2012) such as the whale, the one-sentence warning that converted a whole city down to the animals, and the appearance of God at the end. As Thomas Hobbes put it, life then was solitary, poor, nasty, brutish, and short. Only the sensational broke through their miserable state to capture the imagination of the lay believer. And, to the anonymous author's credit, Jonah is one of the best-known characters in the OT and one of the few cited by Jesus (Matthew 12:38-42; Luke 11:29).

Discernment in the message of Jonah's ministry is in the form of a remarkable satire. The story is brimming with messages for all of us—you and me—who are today's **unprofitable servants (Luke 17:7-10).** Notice that Jesus did not call us worthless servants, but rather unprofitable. Namely, God is always investing more in us than we can ever give in return.

When it comes to unprofitable servants Jonah is the perfect model. He ran from God as soon as God called him and was only thankful that he did not drown and acknowledged none of God's other help. Though named as a prophet of God, he was less perceptive than the sailors! He witnessed to Nineveh with only a one-sentence message that was in one sentence both a warning and a threat rather than an expression of God's care for them. In the end, he was preoccupied with his comfort and selfishly waiting in sadistic longing for Nineveh's destruction rather than rejoicing in their conversion. There is not even any evidence that God's appearance to him had any effect.

However, despite Jonah's abysmal evangelizing, God's word was effective.

Even though the author stated that Nineveh was a city of 125,000 people when the archeologists say it could only have been a city of 10-13,000, God's word was effective. Despite Jonah's immaturity, cowardice, and self-seeking God's word was effective. Even though Jonah hoped Nineveh's destruction would be entertaining, God was as concerned about Nineveh's miseries as angry at its evils. God pitied them because they were so hapless, pointing out to Jonah that the animals were not to blame and the people so wretched that they could not distinguish their right hand from their left!

Yet the message of Jonah is clear that to avoid or resist God's domination is to resist the will of the Father. As for all those who stand apart from God, while we cannot and should not judge them, we must warn them that according to Jesus their situation is perilous.

While we may not feel as alone and faced with impossible odds as Jonah, we can validly be alert to the reality that there is no longer a shared, universal social consensus on virtue. The world has become too divergent and personalistic, too cynical and skeptical, to return to the virtue consensus of the past. However, Catholic psychotherapists who routinely deal with individuals or families can bring images of faith, hope, and love to bolster clients' hopes and struggles.

Competence is an essential applied virtue for psychotherapists that implies an ability to shape individualistic and personal manifestations of the seven virtues. From a psychotherapeutic perspective, in his parables, Jesus manifested competent praxis, an ability to work within an individual's context, attention to the person, acknowledgment of their respective values, and masterful brevity in case presentation.

Accordingly, my hope is this book will be a conversation starter to:

1) Propose spiritual and psychological strength in the virtues as a goal for self and others.

2) Interpret competence as a modern expression of the virtues of prudence, fortitude, and temperance.

3) Relate Jesus' parables as apt expressions of the virtue of justice in outreach to needy clients, especially in Jesus' principle of "publicans and prostitutes over Pharisees and scribes."

4) Trace movement toward virtues as motivation for goal achievement (Niemivirta, Pulkka, Tapola, & Tuominen, Achievement Goal Orientation: A Person-Oriented Approach, 2019) in psychotherapy.

5. Match essential virtue work to psychotherapy (Cessario, Titus, & Vitz, 2013) to foster personal unity, ordered inclinations, reasonable acts, tempered desires, balanced emotions, and tempered strength.

6) Identify Hayes' (2012) seven mindful skills 1) flexibility, 2) seeing with ACT (Acceptance and Commitment Therapy) eyes, 3) developing an ACT relationship, 4) creating a context for change, 5) remaining in the present moment, 6) connecting with values, and 7) committing to action.

7) Name ways in which Hayes's skills echo Jesus' approach to circumstances and people.

8) Find ways in which psychotherapy brings unique resources to therapist and client psychological and spiritual growth and development such as sorting our T-F-A (thinking, feeling, and acting), identifying whose problem something is, estimating levels of

functioning, clarifying diagnoses, understanding developmental stages, and issues, providing insights into personality, sharing a plethora of techniques, and so very much more.

The goal of working our stories is to unveil our minds and hearts so that we can be **the lamp on a stand (Luke 8:16, 11:33-36)** to the world. Therefore, let us resolve and consider:

- Unlike Jonah let us go wherever the Word leads us and not run away as Jonah did.

- The sailors showed more fear of God and insight into Jonah running from God. Let us allow ourselves to learn insight from our clients.

- Even the canticle or song of thanks (Jonah 2:3-10) has nothing to do with Jonah's mission, only that he's thankful he didn't drown. Let us be more thankful in quantity and quality than Jonah in offering frequent thanks and praise for what God is doing in our lives.

- Jonah was saved by miraculous and spectacular fish. Let us recognize when we have been saved and pro-tected by God at key moments.

- Jonah's minimal message was, "Forty days more and Nineveh shall be destroyed." Let our messages to clients be filled with hope, faith, and love. Let us learn to share a bit more of the riches of God's word and message.

- Jonah's ministry was one day or less. Everything else was God getting him to that day and reprimanding Jonah afterward. Let us allow God to lead us to minis-try and guide us afterward often through many years.

- Jonah was blinded by his narrow-minded selfishness, vindictiveness, and secret desire for drama. Let us pray for God to unveil our consciousness and enlighten our minds and hearts.

- Jonah showed no willingness to learn even when God appeared to him. Let us accept our personal need for lifelong learning (Roberto, 2022).

- Jonah was focused on his comfort after his mission. Let us accept the discomforts of our therapeutic tasks, and trust that God's Word will produce fruit in us and others, despite our limitations.

WORKSHEETS

Worksheet #1: ACT's (Acceptance and Commitment Therapy) Six Core Therapeutic Processes		
Replace	With	Goal (Stoddard & Afari, 2014, pp. 7-12)
Experiential avoidance	Acceptance	Willingness to make contact with inner experiences without efforts to escape, change, or control events.
Cognitive fusion	Defusion (unveil)	Stepping back and observing our thinking, feeling, and actions rather than reacting impulsively.
The dominance of the conceptualized past and feared future	Present-moment awareness	AKA mindfulness in traditional religious practice, i.e., non-judgmental, present-focused awareness of degrees of acceptance, defusion, and self-as-context.
Attachment to a conceptualized self	Self-as-context	A sense of self that transcends immediate experiences. Your "you" can observe and experience your inner and outer world so that you are more than your thinking, feeling, and acting.
Lack of clarity regarding values	Values	Individual personal meaningful paths and directions lead to a rich and fulfilling life.
Lack of actions directed toward values	Committed action	Walking the walk so that learning motivates us to clarify values to reach goals.
Psychological inflexibility	Psychological flexibility	"is the ability to be present and open to our experiences so that we can take actions guided by values" for what matters to us ((Stoddard & Afari, 2014, p. 11).

WORKSHEET #2:
TELLING OUR STORIES

Why "our stories?" Psychotherapists make a living listening to stories. Sharing and hearing stories is the "language" through which clients and psychotherapists speak to one another.

As Aslan, the lion, the Christ figure in C.S. Lewis', *The Horse and His Boy (Chronicles of Narnia, #5)*, the hero had asked about someone they met on their adventure, "Child,' said the Lion, 'I am telling you your story, not hers. No one is told any story but their own." So, I invite you to "hear" and, if you choose, to tell your story of your adventure with God. No one can "hear" or tell your story but you. To hear it and tell it is to find God's action, wisdom, and power for holiness in the events of your life.

God knows and loves your story. Do you? Want to understand people today? Then, empathize with their stories. To do that let the Spirit teach you to speak of your story.

I call on you to put aside any fears or embarrassments. Look at your stories as if you were watching a movie of your life: what was good in your story, what was bad in it, and where God was present for you from moment to moment?

How has God been with you in crucial moments or provided what you needed in that time?

Stories (Biesenbach, 2018) cause our brains to produce oxytocin, a chemical related to empathy and a desire to cooperate (p. 12). Stories "get to the heart of it" (p. 14) and put a face on our life story. They connect us, humanize us, accomplish "show, don't tell" (p. 15-6)

Stories (Biesenbach, 2018) force us to consider our audience (p. 28-36), what

1. They want
2. They need
3. They understand

4. They have in common

5. Their doubts, fears, mindsets

6. Their mood, attitudes, and culture

Stories force us to consider others'

7. goals

8. challenges

9. ideal characters

10. resolution.

The emotion in stories humanizes us (p. 42-45) and focuses our hearers and us on:

11. the why or motive of characters.

So,

12. Tap into loyalty: who were you or others loyal to?

13. Appeal to pride: what were you or others proud of?

14. Celebrate your heroes

Therefore, get personal

15. Don't let modesty stop you

16. Don't let fear or embarrassment stop you

In looking at your stories, I ask you to attend to the elements of great stories in your history, thoughts, emotions (Biesenbach, 2018, p. 47). Look back on your life as if you were watching a movie. In anthropology, that's called the objective observer. How did God lead, feed, and use you?

In the story focus (p. 60-67) on:

- one character

- avoid tangents: go in a straight line

- stick to clear turning points

- details: separate the good from the bad

  ° use brief details to set the scene

- ○ offer sensory details to bring a story to life
- ○ simplify dates: be less precise the farther back I go
- ○ omit:
  - proper names
  - precise relationship to characters
  - job titles
  - cut the exposition: start with one brief sentence set-up
- Be ruthless in refining and editing my stories.
  - ○ omit irrelevant details
  - ○ compress the timeline
  - ○ change the order of events

Worksheet #3: About Thinking, Feeling, and Acting (T-F-A)

Cognitive Thinking Distortions, etc. distort our motivation and acting on the great commandment. Look in ACT book for ACT approach to T-F-A

	Thinking	Feeling	Acting
Definitions	using one's mind to consider or reason about something.	an emotional state or reaction	Observable actions of any type
Examples	Thoughts, judgments, constructs	Emotions, what motivates us	What said, done, written
Adults	Tends to act to avoid thinking	Tends to avoid their feelings	Better at thinking than acting and feeling
Children	T-F-A fused and, thus, magic is possible		
Strategies	Stepping back and observing our thinking, feeling, and actions rather than reacting impulsively.		
Fusion	Cognitive (thinking distortions)	Emotional (avoidance)	Action (denial)
Dysfunction	Rationalize, judge, criticize, compare to others	Discount, overlook, avoid, ignore	Ignore implications of our behaviors
Misuse	Emotional reasoning, or own/control other's thinking, cognitive thinking distortions (list)	Avoid unpleasant feelings, try to own/control other's feelings	Act to "solve" feeling & thinking through obsessive or compulsive behavior
Addiction	Not controlling our T-F-A and trying to control other's T-F-A		
Un-fusing (Defusing) results	Truth	Peace	Moral actions
Veiling	Cognitive thinking distortions	Emotional: volatility	Destructive actions
Unveiling	Inspired thinking	Emotional peace	Good, moral, constructive actions
Acceptance	Accepting the reality of our T-F-A and others' T-F-A enables us to hear others and forces us to be responsible for our T-F-A. Such acceptance facilitates the possibility of change and understanding of self and others		
Cognitive fusion	Defusion (unveil)	Stepping back and observing our thinking, feeling, and actions rather than reacting impulsively.	

	Tradition	Priestly	Prophetic	Wisdom/Lay
Worksheet #4: The Three Traditions				
1	Old Testament literature	God's action Abraham-Jesus The Historical books: Pentateuch, Samuel, Kings, Chronicles	The 15 prophetic books that disorient, amaze, and then re-orient	The novella and the wisdom books, e.g., psalms, proverbs, song of songs, Job
2	NT Ministry model	Risen Jesus modeled evangelization to the apostles	Paul's prophetic Call by God, knowledge by Risen Lord and Spirit	The crowd and communities of believers in Catholic letters
3	NT Literature type	The Gospels and Acts	Paul's letters	The Catholic Letters
4	Biblical Type/Models	Christ the Priest, apostolic presence -e.g., Peter and the twelve-	Christ the prophet: A sign of the kingdom to come -e.g., Paul-	Christ the King: laity to transform the world -e.g., Mary, our exemplar-
5	Prayer	Centered on the Eucharist and under the authority and initiative of the priest (Hegy, 2017, p. 50)	Liturgy of the hours, community life, charisms. Monastic practices as model and mode (Hegy, 2017, p. 73)	Images of Joy: music, art, drama, narrative stories (Strawn, 2008). Mary's Rosary as discernment outline.
6	Locus now	Hierarchy and clergy	Monastic or vowed community	Family, the secular world
7	Numbers (Vatican Statistics, 2018) Total Catholics 1.34 billion, (+ 88 million)	Bishops, 5,377, .004%; priests, 414,000, 3%, Deacons .3% 47,500	Religious Order priests: not easily separated out; vowed religious 4.7% 641,667	92%: laity: 1.23 billion
8	Discernment	True to doctrine and church	Disorient, amaze, reorient	A life lived before God
9	Witness and The focus of Christian life	Sacraments, doctrine, fullness of revelation	Faithful pronouncements of God's will. Speak for God in time	Living well before God. Wisdom sayings as a guide for life.
10	Men/women	male hierarchy	Charisms evenly split male and female	Woman often lead
11	How each tradition trains and forms its members.	Priestly/orders many years of academic training and spiritual disciplines	Prophetic/theological, formation within a vowed community.	Wisdom/laity, academics, internships, supervision, continuing education/formation
12	Mode	Public worship and preservation of God's revelation	Respond assertively with God's answer to a current situation	Storytelling and narrative on how to live well before God
13	In trouble when	Priests think their leadership makes them superior	Prophetic not true to their charism to speak truly for God	Wisdom/lay forget God or not present in music, art, narrative

WORKS CITED

Aabram, V. (2021, September 12-25). 3 Reasons Why Young People Gravitate to the Traditional Latin Mass. *National Catholic Register*, p. 15.

ACBS: Association for Contextual Behavioral Science. (n.d.). *ACT Books: Specific Populations; FAP and CFT Books; General Purpose Books on Contextual Behavioral Science.* Retrieved February 2, 2022, from contextualscience.org: contextualscience.org/act_books_specific_populations; general_purpose_books_on_contextual_behavioral_science; fap_and_cft_books

Amador, X. (2012). *I Am Not Sick. I Don't Need Help! How to Help Someone with Mental Illness Accept Treatment: 10th Anniversary Edition.* New York: Vida Press.

Anselme, P., & Robinson, M. J. (2019). Incentive Motivation: The Missing Piece between Learning and Behavior. In K. A. Renninger, & S. E. Hidi, *The Cambridge Handbook of Motivation and Learning* (pp. 163-182). Cambridge, United Kingdom: Cambridge University Press.

Austin, N. (2018, March 9). *Francis: the discerning pope.* Retrieved from Thinking Faith: thinkingfaith.org/articles/francis-discerning-pope

Benedict_XVI, P. (2006, November 6). Address of his Holiness Benedict XVI to the Members of the Pontifical Academy of Sciences. Libreria Editrice Vaticana. Retrieved August 5, 2021, from https://www.vatican.va/content/benedict-xvi/en/speeches/2006/november/documents/hf_ben-xvi_spe_20061106_academy-sciences.html

Benedict_XVI, P. (2010). *Light of the World: The Pope, the Church, and the Signs of the Times: A Conversation with Peter Seewald.* San Francisco: Ignatius Press.

Biersbach, R. (2020). *Catholic Psychotherapy and Faith: Hear the Word: Reflections on Seven Parables of Jesus.* BookBaby.

Biersbach, R. (2021). *The Catholic Psychotherapist and Religious Experience: Theory, Practice, and Witness.* BookBaby.

Biesenbach, R. (2018). *Unleash the Power of Storytelling: Win Hearts, Change Minds, Get Results.* Evanston, IL: Eastlawn Media.

Blomberg, C. L. (2012). *interpreting the Parables, Second Edition.* Downers Grove, Illinois: IVP Academic.

Bock, D. L. (2012). *A theology of Luke and Acts, God's Promised Program Realized for All Nations, Biblical Theology of the New Testament.* Grand Rapids, Michigan: Zondervan.

Bottum, J. (2014). *An Anxious Age: The Post-Protestant Ethic and the Spirit of America.* New York: Image.

Brooks, D. (2021, October 7). *Here's the Mindset That's Tearing Us Apart.* Retrieved from The New York Times: https://www.nytimes.com/2021/10/07/opinion/essentialism-stereo-types-bias.html

Brueggemann, W. (1985). *The Message of the Psalms.* Minneapolis, MN: Fortress Press.

Brueggemann, W. (2018). *The Prophetic Imagination, 40th Anniversary Edition.* Minneapolis: Fortress Press.

Burton, F. (2011). *Fire: The Spark That Ignited Human Evolution.* UNM Press.

Catherine_of_Siena. (1980). *Catherine_of_Siena: The Dialogue.* New York/Mahwah, NJ: Paulist Press.

Center for Applied Research in the Apostolate: CARA. (2015, June 4). *Global Catholicism: Trends and Forecasts.* Retrieved from cara.georgetown.edu: https://cara.georgetown.edu/staff/webpages/global%20catholicism%20release.pdf

Cessario, R., Titus, C. S., & Vitz, P. e. (2013). *Philosophical Virtues and Psychological Strengths: Building the Bridge.* Manchester, New Hampshire: Sophia Institute Press.

Ciarrocchi, J. W. (1995). *The Doubting Disease: Help for Scrupulosity and Religious Compulsions*. New York: Integration/Paulist Press.

Clarke, L. (2009). Football as a metaphor: learning to cope with life, manage emotional illness and maintain health through recovery. *Journal of Psychiatric and Mental Health Nursing, 16*, pp. 486-492. Retrieved June 27, 2021, from http://www.maraserrano.com/MS/articulos/mt_39143507.pdf

Confraternity of Christian Doctrine. (2012). *The New American Bible, Revised Edition*. New York: Harper Collins.

Copenhaver, M. B. (2014). *Jesus is the Question: The 307 Questions Jesus Asked and the 3 He Answered*. Nashville: Abingdon Press.

Corey, R. (2021, December 9). *Why the Biden Presidency Feels Like Such a Disappointment*. Retrieved from New York Times: https://www.nytimes.com/2021/12/09/opinion/joe-biden-political-time.html

DeCaussade, J.-P. (2013). *Abandonment to Divine Providence*. Milwaukee, WI: Catholic Way Publishing.

Dubay, T. (1977). *Authenticity: a Biblical Theology of Discernment*. San Francisco: Ignatius Press.

Dubay, T. (1999). *The Evidential Power of Beauty: Science and Theology Meet*. San Francisco: Ignatius Press.

Duggan, B. (1997). *Precatechumenate Manual, Foundations in Faith*. Thomas Moore Publishing.

Echeverria, E. (2016, April 9). *Chapter 8 of Amoris Laetitia and St. John Paul II*. Retrieved from The Catholic World Report: https://www.catholicworldreport.com/2016/04/09/chapter-8-of-and-st-john-paul-ii/

Edsall, T. (2021, October 6). *Trump True Believers Have Their Reasons*. Retrieved from The New York Times: https://www.nytimes.com/2021/10/06/opinion/trump-voters-2020-election.html

Ellis, P. (1968). *The Yahwist: The Bible's First Theologian: with the Jerusalem Bible text of the Yahwist Saga.* Notre Dame, IN: Fidel Publishers, Inc.

Enright, R. D. (2014). *Forgiveness is a Choice: An Empirical Guide for Resolving Anger and Restoring Hope, 2nd Edition.* Washington, D.C.: American Psychological Association.

Ferrone, R. (2021, September). A Living Catholic Tradition: Pope Francis unifies the Roman Rite. *Commonweal*, pp. 15-17.

Forsyth, J. P., & Eifert, G. H. (2016). *The Mindfulness & Acceptance Workbook for Anxiety: Second Edition, A Guide to Breaking Free from Anxiety, Phobias & Worry Using Acceptance and Commitment Therapy.* Oakland, CA: New Harbinger.

Francis, P. (2021, July 16). *Letter of the Holy Father to the Bishops of the whole world, that accompanies the Apostolic Letter Motu Proprio data "Traditionis custode*.... Retrieved from https://www.vatican.va/: https://www.vatican.va/content/francesco/en/letters/2021/documents/20210716-lettera-vescovi-liturgia.html

Francis, P. (2021, July 16). *TRADITIONIS CUSTODES: APOSTOLIC LETTER, Motu Proprio, On the Use of the Roman Liturgy Prior to the Reform of 1970.* Retrieved from vatican.va: https://www.vatican.va/content/francesco/en/motu_proprio/documents/20210716-motu-proprio-traditionis-custodes.html

Gillispie, C. (2003). A Case Report Illustrating the Use of Creative Writing As A Therapeutic Recreation Intervention in a Dual-diagnosis Residential Treatment. *Therapeutic Recreation Journal, 37*(4), pp. 339-348. Retrieved June 27, 2021, from https://bctra.org/wp-content/uploads/tr_journals/1012-3968-1-PB.pdf

Goldingay, J. (2008). Hermeneutics. In T. Longman III, & P. Enns (Eds.). Nottingham, England: Inter-Varsity Press.

Grant, J. A. (2008). Wisdom and Covenant. In T. Longman III, & P. Enns (Eds.), *Dictionary of the Old Testament: Wisdom,*

Poetry & Writings (pp. 858-863). Nottingham, England: Inter-Varsity Press.

Gregory, B. S. (2012). *The Unintended Reformation: How a Religious Revolution Secularized Society.* Cambridge, Massachusetts: The Belnap Press of Harvard University.

Gurven, M., Rueden, C. v., Massenkoff, M., Kaplan, H., & Vie, M. L. (2012, February 17). How Universal is the Big Five? Testing the Five-Factor Model of Personality Variation Among Forager-Farmers in the Bolivian Amazon. *Journal of Personality and Social Psychology, 2*(February), pp. 354-370. doi:10. 1037/a0030841

Hahn, S. (2002). *First Comes Love: Finding Your Family in the Church and the Trinity.* New York: Image Books, Doubleday.

Haidt, J. (2012). *The Righteous Mind: Why Good People are Divided by Politics and Religion.* New York: Vintage Books/ Random House.

Halloran, K. (2013, July 23). *10 Tips for Understanding and Interpreting the Parables.* Retrieved from Unlocking the Bible: https:// unlockingthebible.org/2013/07/10-tips-for-understanding-and-interpreting-jesus-parables/

Hamilton, J. (2008). Divine Presence. In T. Longman III, & P. Enns (Eds.), *Dictionary of the Old Testament: Wisdom, Poetry & Writings* (pp. 116-120). Nottingham, England: Inter-Varsity.

Hankle, D. D. (2013). Christian Theological Anthropology and its implications for Spiritual Discernment. *The Journal of Christian Healing, 29*(#2, Fall/Winter), 16-28. Retrieved December 28, 2021, from https://www.researchgate. net/publication/261511925_Christian_Theological_ Anthropology_and_its_Implications_for_Spiritual_ Discernment/link/02e7e53474eb776d22000000/ download

Hardin, M. (2020). *Knowing God? Consumer Christianity and the Gospel of Jesus.* Eugene, OR: Cascade Books.

Harrington, W. J. (1969). St. Luke. In R. K. Fuller (Ed.), *A New Catholic Commentary on Holy Scripture* (pp. 986-7021). London: Nelson.

Hayes, S. (n.d.). About ACT. Retrieved August 16, 2021, from https://contextualscience.org/about_act

Hayes, S. (n.d.). ACT Therapeutic Posture. Retrieved August 16, 2021, from https://contextualscience.org/act_therapeutic_posture

Hayes, S. (n.d.). ACT Therapeutic Steps. Retrieved August 16, 2021, from https://contextualscience.org/act_therapeutic_steps

Hayes, S. C., Strosahl, K. D., & Wilson, K. G. (2012). *Acceptance and Commitment Therapy: The Process and Practice of Mindful Change, Second Edition*. New York: Guilford Press.

Hayes, S. (n.d.). Common Misunderstandings About ACT/ RFT. Retrieved August 16, 2021, from https://contextualscience.org/common_misunderstandings_about_act_/_rft

Hayes, S. (n.d.). Criticism: "ACT is Outright Taken from Morita Therapy". Retrieved August 16, 2021, from https://contextualscience.org/criticism_act_is_outright_taken_from_morita_therapy

Hayes, S. (n.d.). Criticisms of ACT. Retrieved August 16, 2021, from https://contextualscience.org/criticisms_of_act

Hayes, S. (n.d.). Functional Contextualism. Retrieved August 16, 2021, from https://contextualscience.org/philosophical_roots

Hayes, S. (n.d.). Getting Beyond the Way of the Guru and Other Scientific Deadends. Retrieved August 16, 2021, from https://contextualscience.org/getting_beyond_the_way_of_the_guru_and_other_scientific_deadends

Hayes, S. (n.d.). Quick & Dirty ACT Analysis of Psychological Problems. Retrieved August 16, 2021, from https://contextualscience.org/quick_dirty_act_analysis_of_psychological_problems

Hayes, S. (n.d.). The Six Core Processes of ACT. Retrieved August 16, 2021, from https://contextualscience.org/the_six_core_processes_of_act

Hayes, S. (n.d.). Theory of Psychopathology. Retrieved August 16, 2021, from https://contextualscience.org/theory_of_psychopathology

Hegy, P. (2017). *Lay Spirituality: From Traditional to Postmodern.* Eugene, Oregon: WIPF & Stock.

Hibbing, J. R., Smith, K. B., & Alford, J. R. (2014). *Predisposed: Liberals, Conservatives, and the Biology of Political Differences.* New York: Routledge.

Ivereigh, A. (2018, October 24). *To Discern and Reform; The 'Francis Option' for Evangelizing a World in Flux.* Retrieved from Thinking Faith: thinkingfaith.org/articles/discern-and-re-form-'francis-option'-evangelizing-world-flux

James, W. (1905, 1997). *The Varieties of Religious Experience: A Study in Human Nature.* New York: Simon and Schuster.

Jeremias, J. (1963). *The Parables of Jesus, Revised Edition.* New York: Charles Scribner's Sons.

John_of_the_Cross. (1979). The Ascent of Mount Carmel, Vol. 2. In John_of_the_Cross, *Collected Works of St. John of the Cross* (&. O. K. Kavanaugh, Trans.). Washington, D.C.: ICS Publications.

Kagan, R. (2021, September 23). *Opinion: Our constitutional crisis is already here.* Retrieved from washingtonpost.com: https://www.washingtonpost.com/opinions/2021/09/23/robert-kagan-constitutional-crisis/

Kaplan, G. (2021, June). A Crisis in Catholic Theology: The uncertain future of theology in the U.S. academy. *America*, pp. 20-25.

Keating, T. (1970). *Crisis of Faith.* Still Water, MA: St. Bede's Publications.

Keating, T. (1994, 2009). *Intimacy with God: An Introduction to Centering Prayer*. New York: Crossroad Publishing.

Keating, T. (2006). *Open Mind, Open Heart: The Contemplative Dimension of the Gospel*. London, England: Bloomsbury Continuum.

Kendall, R. T. (2004, 2006). *The Parables of Jesus: A Guide to Understanding and Applying the Stories Jesus Told*. Grand Rapids, MI: Chosen, Baker Publishing.

Long, J. W. (2018). *Two Existential Theories of Knowledge: Epistemic Pragmatism and Contextualism*. Bloomington, IN: iUniverse.

MacIntyre, A. (1981, 1984, 2007). *After Virtue: A Study in Moral Theory, 3rd Edition*. Notre Dame, Indiana: University of Notre Dame Press.

MacNutt, F. (1974, 1999). *Healing, Revised Edition*. Notre Dame, IN: Ave Maria Press.

Matthews, V. (2008). Social-Scientific Approaches. In T. Longman III, & P. Enns (Eds.), *Dictionary of the Old Testament: Wisdom, Poetry & Writings* (pp. 728-733). Nottingham, England: Inter-Varsity Press.

McEvoy, T. (2020, November 12). *A Time of Choosing: Conversion and Discernment in the Mind of Pope Francis*. Retrieved from Pathwaystogod.org: www.pathwaystogod.org/resources/thinking-faith/tim-choosing-conversion-and-discernment-mind-pope-francis

McFarland, E. (2021). *Blockchain Wars: The Future of Big Tech Monopolies and the Blockchain Internet*. Las Vegas, Nevada: Evan McFarland.

Meninger, W. A. (1996). *The Process of Forgiveness*. New York: Bloomsbury.

Millon, T., & Davis, R. (1996). *Disorders of Personality: DSM-IV and Beyond*. New York: John Wiley & Sons.

Moore, T. V. (1956). *The Life of Man With God*. New York: Harcourt, Brace, and Company.

National Conference of Catholic Bishops. (1988). *Rite of Christian Initiation of Adults (RCIA), Study Edition*. Chicago: Liturgy Training Publications.

National Conference of Catholic Bishops. (2006). *What is original sin? How does it impact me?* Retrieved from NCCB: nccb/original sin/

Niemivirta, M., Pulkka, A.-T., Tapola, A., & Tuominen, H. (2019). Achievement Goal Orientation: A Person-Oriented Approach. In K. A. Renninger, & S. E. Hidi, *The Cambridge Handbook of Motivation and Learning* (pp. 566-616). Cambridge, UK: Cambridge University Press.

Nieuwsma, J. A. (2016). *ACT for Clergy and Pastoral Counselors: Using Acceptance and Commitment Therapy to Bridge Psychological and Spiritual Care*. Oakland, CA: Context Press/New Harbinger.

Ostdiek, G. (2015). *Mystagogy of the Eucharist, A Resource for Faith Formation*. Collegeville, Minnesota: Liturgical Press.

Pentin, E. (2021, September 12-25). Traditional Institutes Seek Mediation over Motu Proprio. *National Catholic Register*, pp. 8-8.

Phillips, E. (2008). Novella, Story, Narrative. In T. Longman III, & P. Enns (Eds.), *Dictionary of the Old Testament: Wisdom, Poetry & Writings* (pp. 492-496). Nottingham, England: Inter-Varsity Press.

Phillips, K. (2006). *American Theocracy: The Peril and Politics of Radical Religion, Oil, and Borrowed Money in the 21st Century*. Viking Adult.

Photios, S. (2005). *The Mystagogy of the Holy Spirit (The Fathers of the Church)*. Brookline, MA: Holy Cross Orthodox Press.

Podrifka, J. (2008). Life, Imagery of. In T. Longman III, & P. Enns (Eds.), *Dictionary of the Old Testament: Wisdom, Poetry*

& *Writings* (pp. 431-437). Nottingham, England: Inter-Varsity Press.

Pokrifa, J. (2008). Life, Imagery of. In T. Longman III, & P. Enns (Eds.), *Dictionary of the Old Testament: Wisdom, Poetry & Writing* (pp. 431-437). Nottingham, England: Inter-Varsity Press.

Pokrifka, T. (2008). Time. In T. Longman III, & P. Enns (Eds.), *Dictionary of the Old Testament: Wisdom, Poetry & Writings* (pp. 820-826). Nottingham, England: Inter-Varsity Press.

Pollan, M. (2013). *Cooked: A Natural History of Transformation.* New York: Penguin.

Pope_Francis. (2016). *The Joy of Love: On Love in the Family.* Wellspring.

Pope_Francis. (2020). *Fratelli Tutti (All Brothers): Encyclical Letter: On Fraternity and Social Friendship.* Cottbus, Germany: Royal Press.

Pope_Francis. (2020). *Let us Dream: The Path to a Better Future: In a Conversation with Austen Ivereigh.* New York: Simon & Schuster.

Purdue, L. (2008). Cult, Worship: Wisdom. In T. Longman III, & P. Enns (Eds.), *Dictionary of the Old Testament: Wisdom, Poetry & Writings* (pp. 78-85). Nottingham, England: Inter-Varsity Press.

Rahner, K. (1975). Original Sin. In K. e. Rahner, *Encyclopedia of Theology: The Concise Sacramentum Mundi* (pp. 1148-1155). New York: Seabury Press.

Ratzinger, J. C. (1997). *Salt of the Earth: Christianity and the Catholic Church at the end of the Millennium: An Interview with Peter Seewald.* San Francisco: Ignatius Press.

Redditt, P. L. (2012). Prophecy, History of. In M. J. Boda, *Dictionary of Old Testament Prophets* (pp. 587-601). Downers Grove, IL: IVP Academic.

Roberto, J. (2022). *Lifelong Faith: Formation for all Ages and Generations.* New York: Church Publishing Incorporated.

Rohr, R. (2001, 2020). *The Wisdom Pattern: Order, Disorder, Reorder.* Cincinnati, OH: Franciscan Media.

Salov, S. (2008, October). *A sourcebook on Solitary Confinement.* Retrieved October 19, 2021, from http://eprints.lse.ac.uk/: http://eprints.lse.ac.uk/24557/1/SolitaryConfinementSourcebookPrint.pdf

Salzman, T. A., & Lawler, M. G. (2018). *Virtue & Theological Ethics: Toward a Renewed Ethical Method.* Maryknoll, NY: Orbis Books.

Sanders, S. (n.d.). *Fruit of the Spirit.* http://sallysanders.com/port-folio/. Retrieved July 2, 2021, from https://www.pinterest.com/pin/29836416253234897/

Sansone, C., Geerling, D. M., Thoman, D. B., & Smith, J. L. (2019). Self-Regulation of Motivation: A Renewable Resource for Learning. In K. A. Renninger, & S. E. Hidi, *The Cambridge Handbook of Motivation and Learning* (pp. 87-110). Cambridge, United Kingdom: Cambridge University Press.

Shields, M. A. (2008). Wisdom and Prophecy. In T. Longman III, & P. Enns (Eds.), *Dictionary of the Old Testament: Wisdom, Poetry & Writings* (pp. 877-884). Nottingham, England: inter-Varsity Press.

Snodgrass, K. (2018). *Stories with Intent: A Comprehensive Guide to the Parables of Jesus, Second Edition, With a new chapter on recent scholarship.* Grand Rapids, Michigan: William B. Eerdmans Publishing Company.

Steinfels, P. (2003). *A People Adrift.* New York: Simon & Schuster.

Sternberg, M. (1985). *The Poetics of Biblical Narrative: Ideological Literature and the Drama of Reading.* Bloomington, IN: Indiana University Press.

Stoddard, J. A., & Afari, N. (2014). *The Big Book of ACT Metaphors: A Practitioner's Guide to Experiential Exercises & Metaphors in Acceptance & Commitment Therapy.* Oakland, CA: New Harbinger Publications.

Strawn, B. A. (2008). Imagery. In T. I. Longman, & P. Enns (Eds.), *Dictionary of Old Testament: Wisdom, Poetry & Writings* (pp. 306-314). Nottingham, England: Inter-Varsity Press.

Strosahl, K., & Robinson, P. J. (2017). *The Mindfulness & Acceptance Workbook for Depression, Second Edition, Using Acceptance and Commitment Therapy to Move Through Depression & Create a Life Worth Living*. Oakland, CA: New Harbinger.

Stuart, D. (2012). Jonah, Book of. In M. J. Boda, & J. G. McConville (Eds.), *Dictionary of the Old Testament Prophets* (pp. 455-466). Nottingham, England: Inter-Varsity Press.

Swoboda, K. (2018). *The Courage Habit: How to accept your fears, release the past, and live your courageous life*. Oakland, CA: New Harbinger.

TerKerst, L. (2020). *Forgiving What You Can't Forget: Discover How to Move on, Make Peace with Painful Memories, and Create a Life That's Beautiful Again*. Nashville, TN: Nelson Books.

The Association for Catechumenal Ministry. (n.d.). *5 Reasons People Don't Stick: Fostering the Full Implementation of the Order of Christian Initiation*. Retrieved January 25, 2022, from acmrcia.org: https://acmrcia.org/blog/5-reasons-people-dont-stick

Tibbits, D. (2007). *Forgive to Live: Devotional, 56 Spiritual Insights on Forgiveness that Could Save Your Life*. Orlando, FL: Florida Hospital.

Trueman, C. R. (2020). *The Rise and Triumph of the Modern Self: Cultural Amnesia, Expressive Individualism, and the Road to Sexual Revolution*. Weaton, Illinois: Crossway.

Tucker, D. (2008). Psalms 1: Book of. In T. Longman III, & P. Enns (Eds.), *Dictionary of the Old Testament: Wisdom, Poetry & Writings* (pp. 578-593). Nottingham, England: Inter-Varsity Press.

Twain, M. (1835, 1910). *Personal Recollections of Joan of Arc, Dover Thrift Edition*. Dover Publications.

United States Catholic Conference. (1995). *Catechism of the Catholic Church, with Modifications from the Editio Typica.* New York: Doubleday.

VanGemeren, W. (2008). Mountain Imagery. In T. Longman III, & P. Enns (Eds.), *Dictionary of the Old Testament: Wisdom, Poetry & Writings* (pp. 481-483). Nottingham, England: Inter-Varsity Press.

Vatican Council II. (1975). Decree on the Apostolate of the Laity. In V. C. II, *Vatican Council and Post Conciliar Documents* (pp. 766-798). Newport, NY: Costello Publishing Company.

Wablen, C. (2008). Wisdom, Greek. In T. Longman III, & P. Enns (Eds.), *Dictionary of the Old Testament: Wisdom, Poetry & Writings* (pp. 742-847). Nottingham, England: Inter-Varsity Press.

Walton, J. H. (2008). Job, Book of. In T. Longman III, & P. Enns (Eds.). Nottingham, England: Inter-Varsity Press.

Watson Institute of International & Public Affairs of Brown University. (2021, August). *Costs of War.* Retrieved from https://watson.brown.edu/: https://watson.brown.edu/costsofwar/costs/human

Wells, B., & Magdalene, R. F. (2008). Law. In T. LongmanIII, & P. Enns (Eds.), *Dictionary of the Old Testament: Wisdom, Poetry & Writings* (pp. 420-427). Nottingham, England: Inter-Varsity Press.

Wenham, D. (1989). *The Parables of Jesus.* Downers Grove, IL: InterVarsity Press.

Wiley, T. (2002). *Original Sin: Origins, Developments, Contemporary Meanings.* New York: Paulist Press.

Wilson, J. (2014). *The Storytelling God: Seeing the Glory of Jesus in His Parables.* Wheaton, IL: Crossway.

Zada, J. (2021). *Veils of Distortion: How the News Media Warps our Minds.* Terra Incognita. Retrieved from johnzada.com